Revise for OCR GCSE Food Technology

Alison Winson

RECOGNISING ACHIEVEMENT

Heinemann Educational Publishers
Halley Court, Jordan Hill, Oxford OX2 8EJ
Part of Harcourt Education

Heinemann is the registered trademark of
Harcourt Education Limited

© Alison Winson, 2003

First published 2003

07 06 05 04 03
10 9 8 7 6 5 4 3 2 1

British Library Cataloguing in Publication Data is available
from the British Library on request.

ISBN 0 435 41715 0

Typeset by Tech-Set Ltd

Original illustrations © Harcourt Education Limited 2003

Printed in Great Britain by The Bath Press Ltd, Bath.

Acknowledgements
Every effort has been made to contact copyright holders of material
reproduced in this book. Any omissions will be rectified in subsequent
printings if notice is given to the publishers.

The author wishes to acknowledge the assistance of Nathalie Bufton,
Barbara Di Nicoli, Michael Winson and John Hill.

Tel: 01865 888058 email: info.he@heinemann.co.uk

Contents

How to use this book

This book has been written as a revision guide for students studying the OCR specification for GCSE in Design and Technology (D&T): Food Technology. It can be used in conjunction with the following OCR resources:

- GCSE Food Technology for OCR student book, which gives more detailed information and coverage of the specification content
- OCR GCSE Design and Technology (D&T): Food Technology specification.

The revision guide covers the content and guidance notes included in the specification. It contains a breakdown of the basic information and knowledge required to ensure that you are better prepared to answer any question set on any aspect of the specification content.

It is also advisable to keep yourself up-to-date with current developments in the relevant technologies, processes and materials by investigating a range of resources from the Internet to the local newspapers.

How this book is set out

Specification links

The panel at the beginning of each section contains a list of the main points covered, reflecting the content and order in the specification.

Key words

The key words related to a particular section appear in panels in the margins and help you focus on and remember the important terms.

Key points

These summaries of the most important points in the section are useful as a quick revision resource.

Activities

The activities at the end of each section will help you:

- practice applying the knowledge you have gathered from the section
- use strategies to re-structure the information and remember it more easily.

Questions

The questions at the end of each section can be answered using the information in that section. To practice for the examination you can either:

- revisit the text to answer the questions
- answer the questions first and then use the text to check your understanding.

Exam Guidance

This section summarises the scheme of assessment and question paper requirements outlined in the OCR specification. It also contains useful tips and guidelines to help you prepare for the written examination.

The GCSE Design and Technology (D&T): Food Technology written examination allows students to demonstrate their specialist knowledge, skills and understanding of textiles technology by answering questions on the subject content outlined in the specification.

Question paper requirements

The combination of question papers you will take for the OCR GCSE in Food Technology depends on the tier of entry you are working on and whether you are taking the full or the short course.

Tier of entry

Papers 1 and 3 – Foundation tier papers, which allow students to achieve Grades G–C. They are both one hour long.

Papers 2 and 4 – Higher tier papers, which allow students to achieve Grades D–A*. They are both one hour and fifteen minutes long.

Full or short course

Full course students complete both the question papers for their tier of entry.

Short course students complete only one question paper from either the foundation or higher tier of entry.

Papers 1 and 2 will include a product analysis question based on information contained in the question paper. The focus of this question will be on a different theme to the one in papers 3 and 4.

Papers 3 and 4 will also contain a product analysis question but on a theme published before the examination. The theme can be researched in advance, but information gathered cannot be taken into the examination.

Structure of the question papers

There are five compulsory questions on each paper and each question is worth ten marks. The questions are divided into sub-sections. The easier questions are at the beginning and they become gradually more difficult towards the end of the paper. The harder questions require more detailed answers, showing more technical knowledge.

Examination technique

A typical question is given below. Lots of tips have been added to help you answer similar questions successfully.

(a) Name the following symbols found on food packages.

....   [3]

(b) Plastic is a popular packaging material.

   (i) Give **two** reasons why plastic is a popular packaging material.

   Reason One...

   .... [1]

   Reason Two...

   .... [1]

   (ii) Give **one** disadvantage of using plastic as a packaging material.

   Disadvantage...

   .... [1]

   (iii) State **one** example of a food product that is packaged using plastic.

   .... [1]

(c) Give **three** reasons why people buy ready made meals.

Reason One ....

....

Reason Two...

....

Reason Three...

.... [3]

Top tips

- Time available to answer each question: 12 minutes for foundation tier and 15 minutes for higher tier.

- Words such as 'list', 'state' or 'name' usually indicate that one-word answers are acceptable.

- Words such as 'identify', 'describe' and 'analyse' usually require a more detailed, structured answer.

- If asked to draw a diagram, you should draw one. Add clear annotation (labels) where required.

- If you are asked to design or draw an item, look at the number of marks allocated for it and include at least that number of features in the design. Some indication of colour will be expected in design questions.

- The marks allocated for each part of the question are a good guide to the amount of detail needed in the answer.

- The amount of space (number of lines) is another clue to how detailed the answer should be. For example, the two lines and the two marks for part **b** indicate that two different answers are needed.

- A product analysis question will always ask you to apply your knowledge to the wider effects of design and technology on society and industrial practice, as well as to show your understanding of the design and make process.

- Spelling is not crucial, but legibility is. Marks are not lost if a word is spelt incorrectly, but they are if the examiner cannot read and understand the answer.

- Remember to use the knowledge you have gained from your internal assessment (coursework) piece. Questions often refer to the design and make process you have actively experienced.

Summary

You need to be thoroughly prepared for the examination as it is worth 40% of your final mark. This means that the recommended time allowance for examination preparation is 26 hours.

Have fun!

Designing and Making

Developing and writing a design brief

This section will cover:

- Identifying design problems.
- Identifying the **user group** or **intended target market**.
- Developing a design brief for a **marketable** product.

Identifying design problems

When a new food product is developed, the first step is to identify a **gap in the market** or a need. There is little point spending time and money developing a new product that no one wants or needs. By carrying out initial research the type of product to be developed and a user group or target market can be identified.

How is the gap in the market identified?

A **food retailer** or a **food manufacturer** often identifies this gap by ...

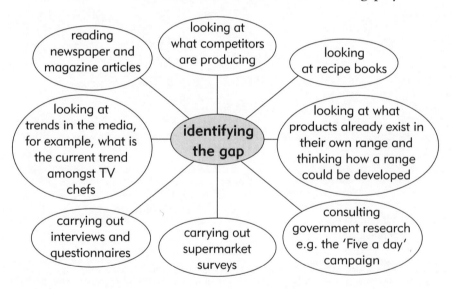

Figure 1: Identifying the gap in the market.

Examples of gaps in the market

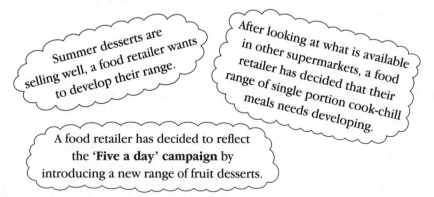

Summer desserts are selling well, a food retailer wants to develop their range.

After looking at what is available in other supermarkets, a food retailer has decided that their range of single portion cook-chill meals needs developing.

A food retailer has decided to reflect the **'Five a day' campaign** by introducing a new range of fruit desserts.

Key words

The **user group** or the **intended target market** is the person or group of people who will use the product, e.g. a single-portion product might be eaten by a single person living alone. Also known as a consumer group.

Marketable: a product is suitable to be sold in a shop.

Gap in the market: before a new product is developed, a retailer or manufacturer has to be sure that there is a need for a new product.

Food retailer: the person who sells the food product.

Food manufacturer: the person who manufactures the food product.

'Five a day' campaign: a campaign launched by the government to encourage people to eat five portions of fruit and vegetables a day.

Identifying the user group or intended target market

It is important to be able to identify the user group or intended target market for a new product if the product is to satisfy a need and become a successful marketable product. The user group or intended target market is the group of people whom a product is aimed at, for example:

- vegetarians
- teenagers
- toddlers
- elderly
- people living on their own
- couples
- parents.

It is important to know who the user group or intended target market will be to ensure the ...

- views of the group are considered
- dietary needs can be taken into account
- eating habits are considered
- preferred cooking method e.g. a teenager might prefer a product that can be cooked in a microwave
- appropriate portion size
- packaging and marketing of the product is focused towards the user group
- cost is appropriate – how much the user group will be able or prepared to pay.

Developing a design brief

Once the initial research has been carried out and the product type and user group have been identified, a design brief can be written. This is a short statement that outlines the problem to be solved.

A completed design brief

'Design and make a marketable hand-held savoury snack for vegetarian adults at a cost of 75p.'

The design brief states

- the product must be marketable
- the type of product to be developed
- the user group or intended target market
- the cost.

Key word

Consumer: the person who buys the food product.

Key points

- Design problems can be identified using a number of sources.
- The user group must be identified and then considered if a product is to be a success.
- A design brief is a short statement outlining the design problems to be solved.

Questions

1 When designing food products it is important to know who the user group or intended target group is. State **two** reasons for this.

2 List **two** ways in which a food retailer or manufacturer might identify a gap in the market.

3 What **four** points would a design brief usually include?

4 Explain what is meant by the 'user group' or 'intended target market'?

Activities

1 Name **one** target group who might buy and use each of the following food products. Give **one** reason for each of your answers.

- frozen luxury pizzas
- ready-made sauces in a jar
- single portion cook-chill lasagne
- frozen four portion shepherd's pie.

2 Below is a list of user groups. Name **one** food product they might buy and give a reason for your answer.

- a parent who has a two-year-old child
- an elderly person living alone
- a student living in a flat.

Drawing up a design specification

This section will cover:

- The intended purpose of a product
- Methods of research
- Issues affecting the development of a new product
- Writing a specification.

The intended purpose of a product

It is important that the **product development team** has a clear understanding of the product's intended purpose. For example:

- The intended purpose of a cereal bar is to provide a quick, hand-held, easy to eat, snack.
- The intended purpose of a single frozen meal is to provide a quick, convenient meal for one person.

Methods of research

Before a manufacturer develops a new product, **research** has to be carried out.

Figure 2: Why carry out research?

Methods of research at this stage might include…

- questionnaires
- evaluating existing products
- supermarket surveys.

Key word

The **product development team** is a group of people who are responsible for creating new food products.

Key word

Research is to use a variety of sources to find out information.

Questionnaires

A questionnaire is a set of questions carefully designed to obtain the opinions of people. Food retailers and manufacturers rarely carry out their questionnaires but instead employ a company to do this for them.

Figure 3: Answering questionnaires.

Questionnaires can be carried out in a variety of ways …

- over the telephone
- in supermarkets
- sent through the post
- on the street.

Evaluating existing products

A food manufacturer may decide to evaluate the existing products of competitors or, indeed, their own products by tasting the product and carrying out **sensory analysis**. Sensory analysis is part of product analysis. It is discussed further in the Knowledge and Understanding unit, in Products and applications (see page 72). A food manufacturer evaluates existing products …

- to get ideas for new products
- to improve existing products.

Supermarket surveys

Visits to supermarkets are useful to find out what products competitors are producing and selling and the costs of similar products. They are also used to find out how well a product is selling. Supermarkets can also provide information about market trends, for example, the eating and shopping habits of people.

Issues affecting the development of a new product

There are several issues that might affect product development at this stage. Here are just a few examples …

1 **Method of production** – the product development team would need to consider if the new product could be manufactured with the existing machinery available. If the answer is no, then often a food production team may have to think again as buying and installing new machinery may be too costly.

2 **Environmental issues** – the retailer may decide that the packaging for the new product should include recycled materials or be recyclable.

3 **Cost issues** – the manufacturer will have to consider how much money is available to produce the new product. This would include the cost of the food materials, the production of the packaging and the product distribution and profit.

4 **Ethical issues** – food retailers and manufacturers may decide that the products they produce will not include any genetically modified foods.

5 **Social issues** – retailers will target certain products to be sold in different areas of the country. Where a product is sold will depend on the type of product and the cost. A luxury product such as a dressed lobster product may only be suitable for a city market where people may have more money to spend on food.

6 **Cultural issues** – this includes the development of products which can be eaten by all cultures, taking into account different religions. For example, a food manufacturer may decide to use vegetarian cheese in food products making it suitable for a wider range of users.

> ### Key word
>
> **Sensory analysis:** looking at, smelling and tasting a food for product development.

Writing a design specification

Once a food manufacturer has carried out research and considered the issues, a **design specification** for a new product can be written. It is usually written as a series of bullet points or a numbered list. A design specification is important because it clearly states the general details of the product to be developed. It is also a checklist for evaluation throughout the development of a product and when testing the final product.

Key word

Design specification: the qualities a product should have.

Example design specification for a savoury low-fat snack product aimed at teenagers

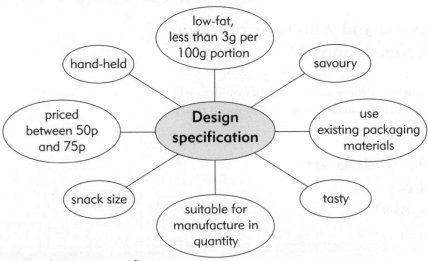

Figure 4: Design specification.

Key points

When designing a new product, the development team needs to make sure:

- that the purpose of the product is clear
- that any research carried out is analysed and used
- cost, environmental, cultural and ethical issues are considered
- a clear design specification is written.

Questions

1 Explain what is meant by the purpose of a product.
2 Why do food manufacturers carry out research? List **two** reasons.
3 State **three** methods of research which may take place whilst a food product is being developed.
4 Explain why a design specification is important when developing new food products.

Activity

1 Write a design specification for each of the following…
   - children's savoury party food
   - healthy snack bar aimed at teenagers
   - adult savoury buffet food.

Generating design proposals

This section will cover:

- What is a design proposal and who is responsible for developing a design proposal?
- How design proposals or ideas are communicated to others.

What is a design proposal and who is responsible for developing the design proposal?

A design proposal is an idea. It is the responsibility of the product development team to develop a design proposal. The number of ideas will depend on the design brief. A specific design brief will usually mean fewer ideas are needed.

How design proposals or ideas are communicated to others

Where do ideas develop from?

- analysis of research information
- existing products
- recipe books
- web sites
- ideas from chefs on the television.

How does a product development team communicate their ideas to other people?

- annotated sketches
- mood boards
- photographs
- making up samples.

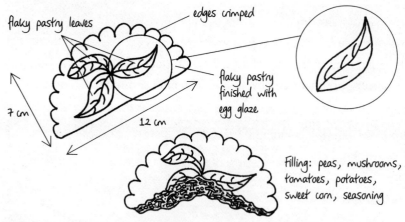

Figure 5: An annotated sketch for a new pastry product.

Figure 6: An example of a food mood board.

Figure 7: Taking photographs.

Figure 8: Making sample recipes.

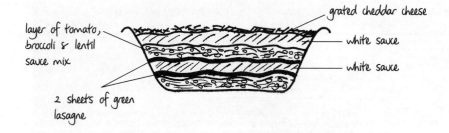

Figure 9: Annotated sketch of a single portion vegetable lasagne.

What should an annotated sketch include?

An **annotated sketch** should include the following elements:

- size/weight
- shape
- ingredients to be used
- finishes
- flavours
- colours
- method of production
- nutritional information.

After gathering together a number of ideas, decisions about which ideas to take forward need to be made. Not all design proposals will become marketed products. These decisions can be made by going back to the design specification and the issues affecting the development of a new product.

Key words

To **annotate** is to label something.

A **sketch** is a rough or quick drawing.

Finishes – a food product is often finished to make it look more appealing, e.g. sprinkled cheese on the top of a shepherd's pie.

Key points

- design proposals can be communicated in a variety of ways
- the specification and issues affecting the development of a new product are used to make decisions about which ideas to take forward.

Questions

1 Below is a design specification for a new cake product.
   - single portion
   - includes buttercream
   - includes icing
   - sponge cake base.

Sketch and annotate your design proposal for the product and explain how you have met the above specification points.

2 The table and star profile below shows the results from sensory analysis testing of a lemon meringue pie.

	Taster 1	Taster 2	Taster 3
attractive finish	1	2	2
pastry – golden colour	2	2	2
sauce – correct consistency	1	1	1
meringue – lightly browned	4	5	4
crunchy meringue	5	4	5
tangy lemon flavour	2	2	3
short pastry	4	5	4
sauce – not too sweet	4	4	4

(5-very good; 3-okay; 1-poor)

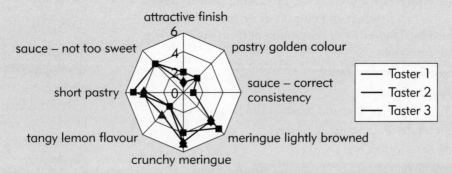

From the results above identify **two** characteristics that need improving and explain how this could be achieved.

3 How might a manufacturer **finish** the following products to make them look more attractive?
- cornish pasty
- lasagne
- sponge cake
- trifle.

4 List **three** ways of communicating ideas when developing a new food product.

Activities

1 The outline below shows the outline of a basic cake shape on a cake board. Using the shape below design a party cake that would appeal to five-year-old children. Ensure that your annotation includes:
- ingredients to be used
- flavours
- colours
- finishes
- size.

Give **three** reasons why your design would appeal to five-year-old children.

2 Draw and complete an annotated sketch of a layered dessert.
- Explain how you might package this product. Give reasons for your suggestions.
- What storage information would you include on the packaging?

Product development

This section will cover:

- Testing and trialling of food products
- The evaluation of a prototype
- Modifying food products
- Writing a product specification
- Costing food products.

Testing and trialling products

Once a product development team have decided which ideas to take forward they begin to make the product on a small scale, producing **prototypes** or samples. They will do this in a **product development or test kitchen**.

When making the product, the product development team must ensure that they keep accurate records by …

- making a list of ingredients and quantities
- costing the ingredients used
- weighing ingredients accurately so that a product can be repeated
- recording the temperature the product is cooked at
- recording how long the product is cooked for.

Figure 10: A test kitchen.

The evaluation of a prototye

Evaluation is ongoing throughout the development of a food product, see 'Product evaluation' on page 53. Once a product development team is

Key words

A **prototype** is the first of its kind produced.

A **product development/test kitchen** is an area within the food factory site where a new product is developed. Recipes are tried out and modified to meet the brief. Domestic and small-scale industrial equipment is used.

satisfied with a prototype, they can begin to ask others to evaluate it. Part of this evaluation will be carrying out **sensory analysis**. This involves:

- looking at the product
- smelling the product
- tasting the product.

Who carries out the sensory analysis?

When a product development team require quick feedback about a product, they will ask other people who work in the food factory to carry out sensory analysis.

However, for more detailed feedback, the general public will be used to carry out sensory analysis. Food manufacturers will often use a set of people who have been chosen and trained because they have very good senses. Often the group of tasters will represent the user group or intended target market e.g. a product aimed at young teenagers would need to be analysed by this user group.

Why carry out sensory analysis?

There are a number of reasons that food manufacturers carry out sensory analysis.

- To test and develop new products
- To improve existing products
- To reduce costs – for example, by changing the cost of a product without changing the taste, texture or appearance
- To allow changes to be made to products before they go into production; this could therefore save time and money, as products are more likely to sell
- To enable the target market to try the product – this will ensure the product is acceptable, or if it is not acceptable, then information can be gained as to how the product could be improved
- To check the quality of a product during production
- To promote a product – this might include tasting panels held in a supermarket.

When would sensory analysis happen?

- Before developing a new product – sensory analysis can be carried out on existing products. Manufacturers can compare their own products with those of competitors
- When a new product has been developed and the team of developers want people's opinions
- During the production process. Samples are taken during the production of products to maintain and check the product is meeting the specification
- At important business meetings. Could be used by the manufacturer when demonstrating the product to buyers
- At the launch or relaunch of a product. This could be carried out in a supermarket to encourage consumers to buy the new or relaunched product.

How can the results of sensory analysis be recorded?

- As a star profile
- On a computer spreadsheet
- In a table.

Why is sensory analysis crucial in industry?

- It keeps the retailer and manufacturer up-to-date with the competition by tasting competitors' products.
- It makes sure a product meets the product specification.
- It enables quality descriptions of a product to be written.
- Quality assurance – to check sensory qualities throughout the design and make process.

What different tests are available when carrying out sensory analysis?

1 **Ranking tests** – these involve placing food products in order. For example, the taster could be asked to place four different beef burgers in order of preference.

Ranking test		Name _____
Please taste the samples and put them in the order you like best.		
sample code	order	comments
○		
□		
△		
■		

Figure 11: A ranking test.

2 **Rating tests** – these involve giving food products a score on a 1–5 scale.

Rating test	○	□	△	■
1 like a lot				
2 like a little				
3 neither like nor dislike				
4 dislike a little				
5 dislike a lot				

Rating score	1	2	3	4	5
sample △					
sample □					
sample ○					

Figure 12: Rating tests.

3 Triangle tests – these are used to see if a taster can tell the difference between food products. For example, can you tell the difference between one brand of cornflakes and another? This test is used if a manufacturer has been asked to develop a similar product to a competitor's.

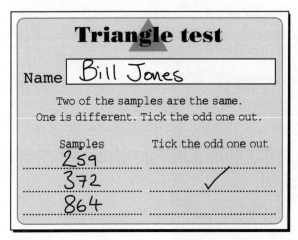

Figure 13: *Triangle tests.*

Sensory describers

These are the words used to describe the appearance, taste, texture and smell of a product, for instance, **mouth-feel** or **consistency**.

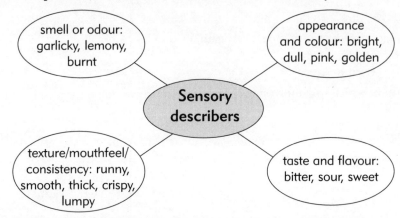

Figure 14: *Sensory describers.*

Carrying out sensory analysis – what has to be ensured?

● The testers must have clear and easy to understand record sheets

● The food should be coded with symbols rather than letters and numbers. Numbers and letters could influence a taster's impressions of a product. For example, 'A' or '1' could be thought to be superior products.

● Tasters should be in individual tasting booths so that others do not influence them

● The same conditions for each taster in terms of the amount of light and temperature within the tasting booth

● The product should be presented in exactly the same way to all the tasters, for example, same-sized portions, same colour of plate

- One sample should be given at a time

- Plain biscuits and/or a drink of water or water and lime should be given between each sample, so that previous flavours don't affect the next product tasted. This is called cleansing the palate

- Products should be given to the tasters at the correct temperature.

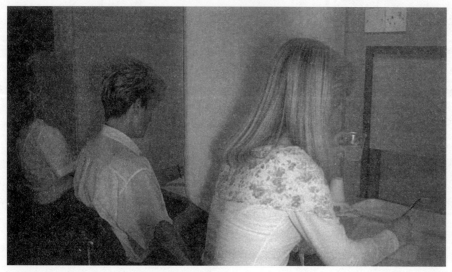

Figure 15: *Tasting booths.*

Modifying food products

Once sensory analysis has taken place, product developers can gather together results and if necessary modify the products.

Food products are modified for several reasons:

- To improve the nutritional content which might involve ...
  - lowering the fat content
  - lowering the salt content
  - lowering the sugar content
  - increasing the fibre content.
- To change the flavour.
- To alter the colour.
- To alter the texture.
- To reduce costs.
- To alter the shape.
- To improve the final appearance of a product.
- To make the product suitable for different dietary and cultural needs.
- To fit packaging design requirements.

Some examples of modifications that can be made to a product are:

- the ingredients used
- proportions of ingredients used
- the cooking method used
- presentation of the product e.g. shape
- assembling of the product e.g. layering differently.

Writing a product specification

Once the product development team are satisfied with the prototype product they have to give careful consideration as to how the new product could be made in quantity. Part of this process will involve writing a **product specification**. The main purpose of a product specification is to make sure that the product can be made many times, and will meet the same standards each time. A product specification may include:

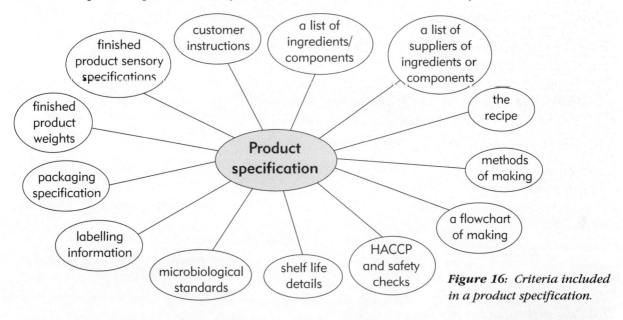

Figure 16: Criteria included in a product specification.

Example product specification

- aimed at 14-16 year olds
- low fat – to contain no more than 5g fat per 100g of finished product
- a savoury product based on pasta, tuna and a roux sauce
- contain a variety of vegetables
- good sensory qualities – tasty, attractive, colourful, appealing, moist
- a ready-made meal
- sold as a single portion of 450g (± 15g) in weight
- quick and easy to cook – i.e. can be reheated in oven or microwave
- sold as a chilled product
- retails at no more than £1.50 when sold as an individual portion
- suitable to add to other ingredients to make a range
- packaged in a paperboard dish which is suitable for reheating in the oven or microwave
- cardboard dish to be vacuum packed in a cellophane bag before being placed in a wax coated cardboard box, so it is easy to dispose of and is light, strong and durable
- packaging that is bright, attractive, shows a picture of the product and displays a low fat symbol
- suitable to be manufactured in quantity.

Key word

A **product specification** is a very detailed list of criteria which the new product must meet. It is much more detailed than a design specification (see page 15).

Costing food products

Costing is an important part of the design process. There is no point in developing a product that will be too costly to produce. It is the job of the product developer to make sure accurate costs are calculated. Costings are calculated using spreadsheets.

The selling price of a food product must take into account …

Figure 17: *The selling price of a food product.*

How do manufacturers lower costs?

Some examples of ways in which some food manufacturers may try to lower costs might include:

- Mixing a more expensive meat with a cheaper one

- Mixing meat with a meat alternative such as textured vegetable protein (TVP)

- Substituting an expensive ingredient with a cheaper ingredient, such as vegetables for meat

- Using flavourings and colourings instead of fresh ingredients, for example fresh fruit

- Making smaller products

- Using extra water in products as a bulking agent. Many products have chemicals added to them to make them hold water, for example chicken products

- Using cheaper packaging materials or using less packaging.

Key points

- Food products are trialled and tested in the product development kitchen.
- Sample products are evaluated using sensory analysis techniques.
- Foods are then modified according to the results of evaluation.

Questions

1 State **one** reason why food samples are coded with symbols rather than letters and numbers when carrying out sensory analysis.

2 Describe the following three sensory analysis tests.

- ranking test
- rating test
- triangle test.

3 Opposite is a recipe for tomato and bacon pasta bake. Give **two** ways in which the fat content can be reduced and **two** ways in which the fibre content can be increased.

Tomato and bacon pasta bake
100g pasta shells
5g crushed garlic
50g chopped onion
200g chopped tomatoes
75g smoked streaky bacon
50g cheddar cheese

4 State **two** ways in which the colour of a macaroni cheese could be improved.

5 Name **one** other method of cooking for each of the following foods that would lower the fat content.

- fried bacon
- fried sausages
- fried egg
- fried chicken
- roast potatoes.

6 Opposite is a recipe for a lasagne. State **one** way in which it could be modified to make it suitable for a lacto-vegetarian.

Lasagne
50g chopped onion
150g minced beef
100g mushrooms
150g canned tomatoes
100g pasta sheets
300ml milk
50g margarine
50g flour
salt and pepper to season

7 State **three** costs that would need to be considered when costing a new food product.

8 Opposite is a recipe for risotto. State **two** ways in which the cost of the product could be reduced.

Risotto
25g finely chopped shallots
50g butter
350g basmati rice
500ml stock (made with a vegetable stock cube)
150g peeled prawns
50g freshly grated Parmesan cheese

Activity

1 When you developed your new product for the coursework, what methods of sensory analysis did you use? How did you record the results? How could you have improved this process? Give reasons for your answer.

2 In your own words describe some changes you have made to food products and give reasons for these changes.

Product planning

This section will cover:

- Producing a detailed plan of work
- Scaling up
- Preparing materials economically.

Producing a detailed plan of work

A plan of work is a detailed list of the stages that need to be worked through to make a product. The product development team would be responsible for writing a plan of work. A plan should include:

- processes to be undertaken
- tools and equipment to be used
- basic **components** or ingredients to be used
- **pre-manufactured standard components** to be used
- time required to cook
- health and safety issues to be considered.

The plan needs to be understood by everyone involved in the manufacture of the food product. The presentation of the plan of work can be in many different forms. Here are two examples:

1 Flowcharts – a flowchart is a diagrammatical way to show a plan of work. A flowchart uses standard symbols.

The standard symbols are

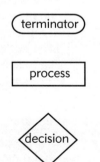

An arrow indicates the direction of flow for the tasks.

A flowchart will also contain 'feedback'. (See page 68.)

(See page 68.)

Key words

A **component** is an individual part of the product, e.g. flour is a component in pastry. Pastry is a component of apple pie.

Pre-manufactured standard components are ready-made ingredients or parts of a product, e.g. a pizza base or a fruit filling for a pie.

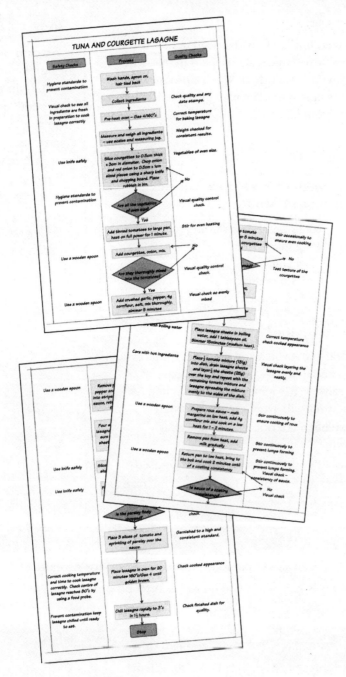

Figure 18: A flowchart.

2 **Process charts** – here is an example of the layout of a process chart.

Stage or task	Processes to be undertaken	Tools and equipment	Basic ingredients	Standard components	Time required	Health and safety

Scaling up

When a recipe has been trialled and is acceptable it would need to be 'scaled up' ready for making in quantity. Usually the large-scale recipe is in the same proportions as the recipe developed in the test kitchen. When a product is ready for the mass production stage, a plan is drawn up. The plan must be detailed and easily understood by all those people involved in its production.

For example:

Fruit scones

Ingredients for a single batch of fruit scones	Ingredients for 500 batches of fruit scones
200g self-raising flour	100kg self-raising flour
50g margarine	25kg margarine
50g sugar	25kg sugar
125ml milk	62.5 litres milk
25g dried fruit	12.5kg dried fruit

Preparing materials economically

Preparing materials economically means that you avoid wastage. Unnecessary waste will make a product more expensive because all materials have to be paid for. The creation of waste also raises environmental and recycling issues.

Examples of how a food manufacturer will avoid creating waste:

- biscuit dough – once shapes have been cut out, excess dough is collected, re-rolled and used again
- excess chocolate used to coat biscuits and icings on cakes is re-used
- cake crumbs from cooked cakes are added back to a raw cake mixture as a bulking agent.

Key points

- Accurate 'scaling up' of ingredients allows sample food products to be mass-produced.
- Being economical with ingredients is important when producing food products.

Questions

1 What do the following symbols represent when used on a flowchart?

2 State **two** ways in which a food manufacturer could avoid wastage when manufacturing a food product.

3 Explain the term 'scaling up'.

Activity

1 Produce a simple flowchart using the standard symbols to show the manufacture of a cheese and tomato sandwich.

Tools and equipment

This section will cover:

- The tools and equipment used in the food industry
- Using tools and equipment safely and hygienically.

The tools and equipment used in the food industry

There are a variety of tools and equipment available in the food industry for carrying out the tasks shown in the diagram.

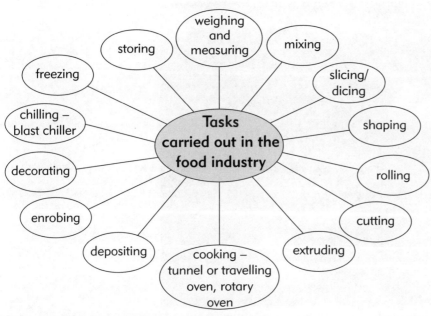

Figure 19: Tasks carried out in the food industry.

Machines in the food industry can be linked to a computer, this is known as **Computer-Aided Manufacture (CAM)**. (See page 42.)

The effects of using machinery

- large amounts can be produced at any one time
- produces a consistent product
- controlled by computer or by people
- produces food products quickly
- fewer workers needed
- highly trained computer operatives needed.

Key word

Computer-Aided Manufacture (CAM) is a process in which machinery is controlled by computers.

A rotary moulder.

Decorating.

An enrober coating chocolate biscuits.

Figure 20*: Examples of large-scale equipment used in the food industry.*

The table below shows a comparison of equipment used in a product-development kitchen and equipment used to manufacture products on a large scale.

Product development kitchen	Large-scale manufacture
digital weighing scales	computer-controlled weighing or measured into hoppers
slicing vegetables using a knife	automatic slicer fed from hopper
peeling potatoes with a peeler	mechanical peelers with specially lined drum
rolling out dough with a rolling pin	dough is sheeted using rollers
shaping dough using hands, cutters, spoon, templates, piping bag	dough is cut using rollers with blades or pressed using moulds
pureeing in a food processor	enormous liquidiser used
cooking in a saucepan	large Bratt pans used
cooking in an oven	computer-controlled travelling or tunnel ovens or rotary ovens
cooling on a wire rack	blast-chilled in cooling tunnels
cutting dough into portions with a knife	automatic cutting
portion controlled with spoon measure	squeezed out with a depositor
using a food probe for temperature control	sensors are computer-controlled
mixing in a bowl or processor	giant mixing-systems used
piping bag for cream	injector or depositor
piping bag for biscuits	depositing machine

Using tools and equipment safely and hygienically

In the food factory staff need to make sure they follow all the following guidelines for health and safety.

Safety

Staff must…

- be trained how to use machines correctly
- have correct footwear, in some circumstances this would need to be protective
- wear clean protective clothing
- tie long hair back and/or cover it with a hair net
- remove all jewellery
- wear eye protection
- wear no loose clothing
- make checks on machinery before using it.

Figure 21: A safe outfit.

33

Hygiene

Staff should…

- have food hygiene training e.g. the **'Foundation level certificate in food hygiene'**
- beards covered by a beard net or snood
- cover all cuts and grazes with a **blue waterproof plaster**
- wash hands with bacterial soap and hot water
- dry hands with hot air drier or disposable paper towels
- wear disposable gloves whenever possible for handing food
- report any illness to a supervisor
- never cough, spit or sneeze over food
- not chew or smoke whilst working
- not wear perfume
- not taste food or lick any equipment e.g. spoons
- keep fingernails short and scrubbed
- not wear nail varnish.

Key word

'Foundation level certificate in food hygiene' is a qualification aimed to improve the knowledge and understanding of food handlers. Areas that are covered by the certificate include personal hygiene, waste and pest control and food storage.

Key word

Blue waterproof plasters are used in the food industry as they can be easily seen if they fall into a food product. They also contain a metal strip which can be detected when the product is passed through a metal detector.

Key points

- Large-scale specialist machinery is used to mass-produce food products.
- There are a number of safety and hygiene rules to follow when using tools and equipment in the food industry.

Questions

1 How is a mass-produced chocolate biscuit coated in chocolate? State **one** method.

2 State **two** effects an increased use of computer-controlled machinery will have on the workforce of a food factory.

3 Compare the tools and equipment that would be used to make a cake in a product development kitchen with the tools and equipment that would be used in the mass production of cakes.

Application	Product development kitchen	Mass production or food factory
weighing and measuring ingredients		
mixing the cake mixture		
placing cake mixture in tins		
baking the cake		
cooling the cake		

4 State **two** reasons why blue waterproof plasters are used in the food industry.

Processes

- Why use food-processing techniques?
- Processing techniques used in the food industry:
  - assembling products
  - heat and chill application
  - food preservation.

Why use food-processing techniques?

Food processing involves making changes to raw materials. Food processing will improve the following qualities of a product:

- **palatability**
- keeping properties
- appearance
- texture
- nutritional value
- ease of preparation.

Processing techniques used in the food industry

There are a number of different processing techniques used in the food industry. Here are some examples:

- assembling products
- heat and chill application
- food preservation
- finishing techniques
- combining one or more ingredient(s).

Three processing techniques will be considered in greater detail:

- **assembly**
- heat and chill application
- preservation methods.

Assembly

Fitting together the parts of a food product e.g. bread and sandwich filling. A series of processes may be required for a fully assembled product.

Heat and chill application

1 **Heat** is used for a variety of reasons in the processing of food products.
   - to increase the **shelf life** of a product
   - to destroy **micro-organisms** and **enzymes**, making food safe to eat
   - to soften food to make it more edible e.g. rice
   - to produce the desired consistency e.g. sauces
   - to improve flavour e.g. potatoes
   - to increase the variety of food products available.

Key word

Palatability is the acceptability of the taste and texture of food.

Key words

Assembly means putting ingredients together to make a food product .

A food product's **shelf life** is how long it can be kept safely and remain of high quality.

Micro-organisms are tiny life-forms. Bacteria, moulds and yeasts are all micro-organisms.

Enzymes are proteins which speed up chemical reactions.

Methods of heat application which are used in the food industry include:

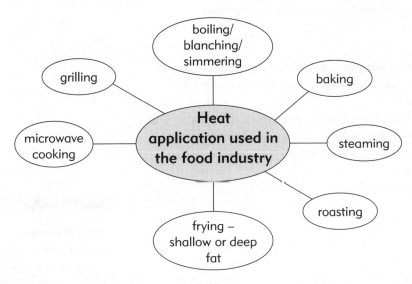

Figure 23: Heat application in the food industry.

Other heat treatments include

- pasteurisation
- sterilisation
- ultra heat treatment (UHT)
- **modified atmosphere packaging (MAP).**

2 **Low temperatures** are used to:
  - increase the shelf life of a product by slowing down enzyme activity and preventing micro-organisms from growing
  - create a wider variety of products available to the consumer.

The two main processing techniques which create low temperatures are freezing and chilling.

Freezing – freezing involves using very low temperatures. Freezing will prolong the shelf life of a product for up to one year. **Blast freezing** is used in the food industry as a method of freezing food quickly. Freezing foods quickly means that smaller ice crystals are formed, causing little damage to the food. Slow freezing will produce large ice crystals and will cause damage. In the food industry temperatures of between –18°C and –29°C are used.

At these temperatures micro-organisms will stop growing and enzyme activity will be slowed down.

Supermarkets operate freezers at between –18°C and –20°C. Frozen products include vegetables, meat, desserts, bread and **cook-frozen** ready meals.

Chilling – chilling will extend the shelf life of a product by a few days. Blast chilling is used in the food industry as a method of chilling food quickly by blasting it with cold air. Blast chilling is used on products such as sandwiches, desserts, **cook-chill** ready meals, and cooked meats.

Key words

MAP, modified atmosphere packaging is the alteration of the atmosphere around the food by adding gases such as carbon dioxide, nitrogen or oxygen.

Blast freezing means super-quick freezing.

Cook-frozen refers to food that has been cooked, fast frozen and then stored at below freezing point.

Blast chilling refers to food that has been chilled quickly by blasting with cold air.

Cook-chill refers to food that has been cooked, fast chilled in $1\frac{1}{2}$ hours and then stored at low temperatures.

Supermarkets will chill foods such as fresh fruit and vegetables. Chilled food is kept at temperatures between 5°C and 8°C. At these temperatures micro-organisms do not multiply as quickly as at room temperature.

Food preservation

Food preservation is a way of increasing the shelf life of a product. If food is not preserved it will deteriorate. This deterioration of food is caused by micro-organisms and by enzymes.

Food preservation methods work on two basic principles. They either destroy micro-organisms and enzymes and thus make food last longer, or they take away the conditions micro-organisms need to multiply (warmth, moisture, nourishment and time).

The principal methods of preservation are:

- **dehydration**
- freezing
- irradiation
- chemical.

> **Key word**
>
> **Dehydration** or drying is the removal of water from a food.

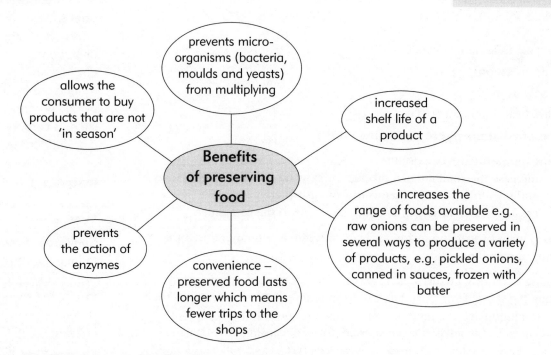

Figure 24: There are many benefits of preserving food.

Limitations – what are the limitations of preserving food?

- The texture of a food may change, e.g. canned strawberries are much softer than fresh strawberries.
- Additives may need to be added to restore colour, flavour and texture of a food product.

Methods of preservation – the table below gives a description of the different methods of preservation used, the limitations and benefits of each method and examples of foods.

Methods	Description	Benefits	Limitations	Example food
Freezing	Low temperatures are used, usually −18°C or below	Nutritional content mainly unaffected. Colour and flavour of foods is generally not affected	Texture can be altered due to cell damage especially in soft fruits	Vegetables, meat, fish, bread, desserts
Canning	Food is placed in can and liquid is added. Can is sealed and then heated at high temperatures	Foods have long shelf life	The texture of some foods will alter e.g. strawberries become soft	Vegetables, fruit, meat, fish, soups, sauces
Drying (Dehydration)	Water is removed from food	Foods are less bulky and weight is reduced which means foods are easier to transport	Foods must be stored in a cool, dry place. Colour, texture, flavour and nutritional content of foods may be affected	Vegetables, fruit, rice, pasta
Accelerated freeze dried (AFD)	Food is frozen and dried	Foods keep their flavour and colour. Little or no alteration to the nutritional content	More costly than simply drying foods. Foods can become brittle so need careful handling	Instant coffee granules, soups
Modified atmosphere packaging (MAP)	The atmosphere around the food is altered by adding gases such as carbon dioxide, nitrogen, and oxygen	The colour of the food will remain the same until the pack is opened. Can see the product. Increased shelf life	Once opened food has a normal shelf life	Meat, fruit, fish, bread, vegetables
Vacuum packaging	Removal of air from a product's packaging	Foods maintain colour and texture	Once opened food has a normal shelf life	Meat, vegetables, fish
Irradiation	Rays are passed from a radioactive beam source through the food, which reduces the number of micro-organisms	Kills insects, delays ripening and sprouting in fruit and vegetables. Destroys micro-organisms	Consumers opposed to method because of the use of radioactive rays. No way of detecting how many times and what dose of irradiation has been given. Loss of nutrients particularly Vitamin C	Fruit, vegetables, prawns, spices

Other methods of food preservation – chemicals are also used to preserve food.
They remove water from the food so that micro-organisms cannot multiply.

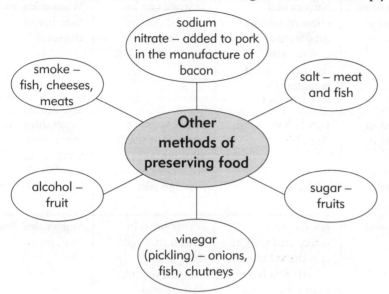

Figure 25: Other methods of preserving food.

Key points

- Food is processed in a variety of ways in the food industry. Examples include assembling food products, application of heat and cold, food preservation and finishing techniques.
- Food preservation is used to prolong the shelf life of products.
- There are many methods of food preservation including freezing, canning, irradiation, AFD, MAP and dehydration.

Questions

1 State **three** benefits of food preservation.
2 State **one** benefit and **one** limitation of accelerated freeze-drying as a method of preservation.
3 At what temperature should frozen food be stored in the supermarket?
4 At what temperature should cook-chill products be stored in the supermarket?
5 State **two** methods of preserving for each of the following foods:
   - meat   - potatoes   - fish   - apples.
6 Give **two** reasons why many consumers prefer to buy cook-chill products rather than frozen.
7 Give **two** reasons why cook-chill products are ideal for elderly consumers.

Activities

1 The following are all heat treatments, which can be used to preserve milk. Find out the differences between each heat treatment.
   - pasteurisation   - sterilisation   - ultra-heat treatment   - irradiation.
2 How could the following foods be preserved? Think of two methods for each food. Meat, fish, eggs, cheese, carrots, onions, apricots, mushrooms, apples, tomatoes and milk.

ICT applications

> ### This section will cover:
> - What is ICT?
> - How are computers used in the food industry?

What is ICT?

ICT (or information communications technology) is the use of electronic devices such as computers, fax machines, and the Internet. ICT is used in the food industry in the development and manufacture of products.

How are computers used in the food industry?

Designing

Computer-Aided Design (CAD) is used in the food industry in many ways:

Example of CAD	Application
Desk-top publishing	Designing surveys/questionnaires. Artwork 3D virtual reality products
Word processing	Creating questionnaires
Internet	To find out about competitors' products
E-mail	Send reports/photographs concerning a new product between the food retailer and the food manufacturer
Graph programs	To produce results of questionnaires/sensory analysis
Nutrition programs	To calculate the nutritional value of a product
Spreadsheets	To calculate costs, analyse the results of surveys/sensory analysis, forecast sales
Paint/draw programs	Produce packaging nets, labelling, artwork on packaging
Digital camera	Provide images for packaging. Recording how a product should look to ensure consistency between products
Clipart	Create mood boards
Scanner	Scanning images onto food packages

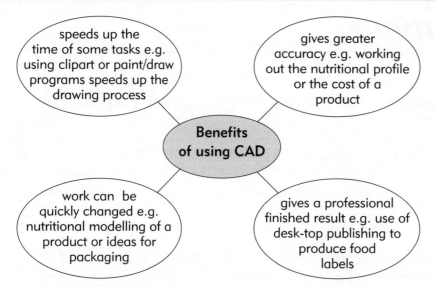

Figure 26: Benefits of using CAD.

Manufacture

Computer-Aided Manufacture (CAM) is also widely used in the food industry. There are many machines in the industry that are controlled by computers.

The photographs on page 32 show a range of computer-aided machinery carrying out various functions such as:

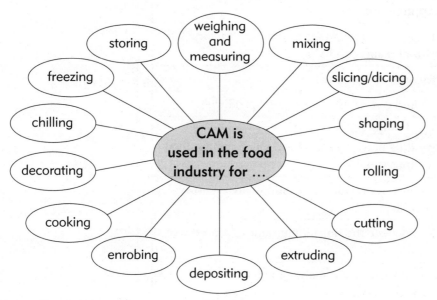

Figure 27: CAM is used to carry out these functions.

Other aspects of the manufacturing process are also dependent on CAM. Some examples include:

- data loggers. These are electronic sensors which will detect and record weight, temperature, colour, pH and moisture changes in a product
- the manufacturing of the packaging
- printing labelling information onto food packages
- stock control.

Some benefits of using CAM include the following:

- It saves time. Repetitive tasks can be completed quickly, for example, when filling pastry cases.
- It also increases productivity. More products made at speed means lower costs.
- Using CAM, a consistent final product is manufactured.
- It increases safety since machinery rather than workers can carry out the more hazardous tasks.

Key points

- Computers are used in a variety of ways in the food industry.
- Computers are used for designing (CAD). Examples include: nutritional analysis, spreadsheets for costing and paint/draw packages for producing packaging.
- Computers are used in the manufacture of food products (CAM). Examples include: data loggers,machinery linked to computers to perform a variety of tasks such as weighing, mixing, shaping, cooking.

Questions

1 What is meant by the letters CAD and CAM?
2 Give **two** examples of how CAD is used in the development of a new food product.
3 Give **two** examples of how CAM is used in the manufacture of a new food product.
4 State **two** benefits of using CAD and **two** benefits of using CAM.
5 What tasks do the following pieces of equipment perform?
   - enrober
   - depositor
   - data logger.

Activities

1 Write a short paragraph to explain how CAD is used in the food industry.
2 Write a short paragraph to explain how CAM is used in the food industry.
3 How did you use ICT in your coursework?

Industrial applications

This section will cover:

- Commercial production methods
- Systems to control food production
- Packaging food products
- Promoting food products.

Key words

Job/craft/one-off production is the production of only one product.

Batch production: a specific amount of a product is manufactured.

To **mass produce** is to produce products in quantity. Examples include repetitive flow, assembly line and continual/ continuous flow production methods.

Commercial production methods

Several production methods are used in the food industry. The method used depends on the food product being produced.

The table below lists:

- the names of different methods of production
- a brief description of the method
- the limitations and benefits of each method
- examples of food products produced by each method.

Method of production	Description	Benefits	Limitations	Examples of products
Job/craft or **one-off**	One product is manufactured.	A high-quality product which is unique.	Products are expensive. Products take time to manufacture. Skilled staff required.	Wedding cake, birthday cake.
Batch	Small numbers of identical or similar products are manufactured.	Small orders can be made. A variety of products can be made. Production costs are cheaper than in job production. The same machinery can be used to make a variety of products.	May be expensive to set up and maintain the factory. Waste is high if the process fails.	Cakes, biscuits, bread, pies, handmade chocolates, cheese.
↓ The following two methods are all examples of **Mass Production** ↓				
Repetitive flow or **Assembly line**	Large numbers of identical products are manufactured on an assembly line.	Large numbers of a product can be manufactured at a low cost. Identical products can be made. Orders can be quickly met.	Can be labour-intensive so staff costs may be high. Many of the tasks that staff carry out are repetitive.	Sandwich production, digestive biscuits, white-sliced loaves.

Method of production	Description	Benefits	Limitations	Examples of products
Continual or Continuous flow	Computer-controlled. One specific product is manufactured 24 hours per day, 7 days a week.	Inexpensive to run. High-quality product. Small workforce needed. A consistent product is manufactured.	Expensive to set up and maintain the factory. If production line breaks down production is stopped. Low labour costs.	Soft drinks, margarine, milk.

Just in time

Just in time refers to an ordering and production system. Manufacturers order food products and/or ingredients when they are needed. This means that they do not have large amounts of food to store. It also means that a manufacturer can quickly change the product they are making without having to use up stock first, saving them money.

Logistics

Logistics is the process of moving ingredients, components and products to the correct place as and when they are needed. This involves the movement of goods into and out of the factory. A delay can mean that time, money and product can be wasted. This means that food manufacturers and food retailers need to have an efficient ordering system.

Systems to control food production

Control systems (see page 67 in the Knowledge and Understanding unit).

What needs controlling?

- size and shape
- temperature – monitored and maintained
- microbial growth
- safety.

Packaging food products

The packaging for a product is developed during the product development stage. The reason for this is to ensure that the whole product can be produced. There would be little point in producing a new food product if it could not be packaged appropriately. The packaging needs to be trialled to make sure it is suitable for the food it will contain.

Why is food packaged?

- to protect the food from being damaged
- hygiene – keeps **micro-organisms** and dirt away from the food
- persuades the customer to buy the product
- makes the food easier to transport
- to provide information to the **consumer**.

Key words

Repetitive flow production involves large numbers of identical products being manufactured.

Continual/ Continuous flow production is computer-controlled. It means that products can be made 24 hours per day, 7 days a week.

Key words

Micro-organisms include bacteria, moulds and yeasts.

The **consumer** is the person who buys and/or uses a product.

Packaging materials

A variety of materials can be used to package food products, as the table below shows.

Packaging material	Benefits	Limitations	Example of food
Glass	Strong, transparent, recyclable, withstands high temperatures, used in microwave.	Heavy, breakable, cannot be easily seen in a product when broken.	Cook in sauce, mayonnaise.
Metals including foil and cans	Withstands high temperatures, lightweight, recyclable, strong.	Cannot be used in the microwave, cannot see the contents, can react with the food so additional non-metallic lining is added.	Canned vegetables and fruit, ready meals.
Plastics	Used in the microwave, easy to print on, inexpensive.	Can be difficult to dispose of.	Yoghurts, ready meals, cheese, bread.
Ovenable paperboard	Used in oven, used in microwave, easy to print on.	Loses its strength and shape when soggy, can easily be squashed and damage product.	Frozen meals, chilled meals.
Paper/card	Recyclable, easy to open, inexpensive, thickness varies, can be printed on, variety of shapes, can be laminated.	Can tear easily, not waterproof, uses natural resources, can be squashed and damage product.	Cereals, sugar, flour.

Figure 28: A selection of packaging materials.

Labelling on packaging

There are certain legal requirements that packaging must fulfil. A food package has to include some information by law. The table below shows what information must be included on a package by law and states reasons why.

Information	Reason
Quantity	Different products can be compared for value for money. Some products do not have to include the quantity, e.g. a loaf of bread.
Ingredients list	Consumer knows exactly what ingredients are contained in a product. Ingredients are listed in weight order, with the largest amount of ingredient first.
Manufacturer's name and address	Product can be returned if faulty or letter of complaint can be made in writing.
Product name	Identifies the product.
Product description	It may not be clear from the product name what the product is.
Date code	Informs the consumer of the length of time the product can be kept. See below.
Storage instructions	Informs the consumer how to store the product.
Instructions for use	Informs the consumer how the product should be used. This includes cooking and heating instructions.

Tamper evident packaging

This is included on many food products. It allows the consumer to check that a food product has not been opened. Examples include a plastic tear-away strip on foods such as milk, and plastic seals on foods such as tomato ketchup.

Figure 29: *Examples of tamper evident packaging.*

Date codes

- The **'best before'** date appears on foods with a short to medium shelf life such as bread, biscuits, crisps and sweets. The day, month and year will be shown.

- The **'use by'** date is found on chilled products e.g. sandwiches, cook-chill meals. The product must be used by the date stated. If it is not used by this date it should be thrown away. The day and month will be shown.

- The **'display until'** date is for the food retailer. Once this date has passed the food product should be removed from the shelf.

Other information found on food packaging

Information	Reason
Nutritional information	Comparisons of the nutritional content of different products can be made.
Serving suggestions	Give the consumer ideas of what could be served with a product.
Cost	The consumer can make comparisons based on cost of different products.
e	Average weight/quantity.
Bar code	Is a way of identifying a product.

Food manufacturers will also include a range of symbols on the labelling of a food package. Here are just a few examples:

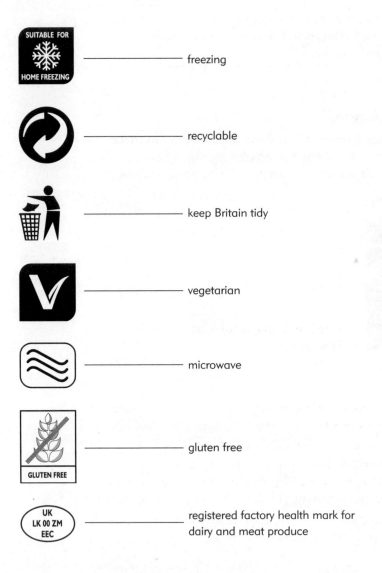

freezing

recyclable

keep Britain tidy

vegetarian

microwave

gluten free

registered factory health mark for dairy and meat produce

Key word

e **symbol** indicates the average weight/quantity of a product.

Each food product has a unique **bar code**, which identifies a product. Bar codes help consumers by providing a quicker service at the till and providing an itemised receipt which can easily be checked. Bar codes help retailers to keep a check of stock and allow faster reordering from the manufacturer.

Additives

Additives are included in food products for many different reasons. Additives can be *natural* or *artificial*. The table below shows the type of additives added, the reasons for inclusion and examples.

Additive type	Reason for inclusion	Examples
Preservatives	To make products last longer by protecting against the growth of micro-organisms.	Salt, sugar, vinegar, sulphur dioxide.
Colours	To improve or change the appearance. To replace colour lost through processing methods.	Beetroot red (**E162**), caramel (E150), tartrazine (E101).
Flavours and flavour enhancers	To improve or change the flavour. To replace flavours lost through processing methods.	Vanilla, sugar, saccharin, aspartame, monosodium glutamate.
Emulsifiers and stabilisers	To improve the texture. To stop foods separating.	Lecithin, xanthan gum.
Antioxidants	To make foods last longer. To stop fatty foods from going **rancid**.	Vitamin C (ascorbic acid). Vitamin E (tocopherol).

Other additives

Additive	Reason used	Example
Raising agents	Used to give a lighter texture to baked products.	Sodium bicarbonate.
Anti-caking agents	Stops powders and crystals sticking together. Added to flour.	Calcium silicate.
Flour improvers	Helps to make bread dough stronger and more elastic.	Ascorbic acid.
Thickening agents	Used to form a gel to thicken sauces.	Modified starch. Guar gum (E412)
Nutrients	Enrich the nutritional value of a food product.	Vitamins and minerals.
Gelling agents	Used to make food set, e.g. jams and jellies.	Pectin

Benefits and limitations of inclusion of additives in food products for the food manufacturer

Benefits	Limitations
Produces a wide range of food products.	Can be used to disguise inferior ingredients e.g. flavours and colours in meat products.
Keeps food safe for longer by protecting against the growth of micro-organisms.	Some colours and flavours may not be necessary in a product.
To improve the colour, flavour, texture of a product.	Some consumers may have an allergy to an additive.
To restore original characteristics of a product e.g. canned peas are grey in colour after being processed. Green colouring is added to the peas as consumers expect peas to be green.	Adds to the cost of a product.
Helps maintain consistency in mass production e.g. use of emulsifiers to ensure ingredients in products do not separate.	Some consumers avoid food with additives.
To produce expected qualities in foods e.g. a dessert mix with yellow colouring and lemon flavouring.	

Benefits and limitations of inclusion of additives in food products for the consumer

Benefits	Limitations
A wider variety of food products is available.	Consumers may not buy a product because it may have an additive they object to e.g. vegans oppose the use of cochineal.
Can increase nutritional value e.g. vitamins added.	In some people can cause allergic reactions/people may have an intolerance.
Food lasts longer so don't need to go shopping as often.	Can be used to disguise inferior ingredients.
Makes food safe by protecting against the growth of micro-organisms.	Some colours and flavours may not be necessary.

Promoting a new food product

New food products are promoted to make sure that consumers are aware that the product is available and that they will buy it.

How might a food manufacturer promote a new product?

- adverts on television, in newspapers, magazines
- sponsorship
- leaflet distribution to homes and in the streets
- free samples through the letterbox, in magazines, in supermarkets
- money off products
- 'buy one get one free' offers.

Key points

- Commercial methods of food production include job, batch, repetitive flow and continual flow.
- Systems are put in place to control size, shape, temperature, safety and hygiene.
- When a food product has been accepted for production, packaging and labelling for the product is developed.
- Food products are promoted in a variety of ways to increase consumer awareness.

Questions

1 Describe each of the following methods of production and give an example of the type of product that would be suitable for manufacture using this method.
    - job/craft or one-off production
    - batch
    - repetitive flow
    - continuous flow.
2 A small local bakery has been asked to make a batch of 50 cheese scones. How will you ensure that they are identical? State **three** ways.
3 State **two** benefits of a bar code.
4 Explain the differences between a 'best before' and a 'use by' date code.
5 Look at the food package below. Whom is the product aimed at? Give **two** reasons for your answer.

6 Below is the nutrition table found on a broccoli and Cheddar cheese quiche.

NUTRITION		
Typical Values	Approx per quiche	per 100g
Energy	1697 kJ (407 kcal)	1130 kJ (271 kcal)
Protein	11.6g	7.7g
Carbohydrate	29.7g	19.8g
of which sugars	2.1g	1.4g
Fat	26.9g	17.9g
of which saturates	14.6g	9.7g
Fibre	2.9g	1.9g
Sodium	0.4g	0.3g
Salt equivalent	1.0g	0.7g

NUTRITION			
EACH DAY	Approx per serving	Women	Men
Calories	407 kcal	2000	2500
Fat	26.9g	70g	95g
Salt	1.0g	5g	7g

Answer the following questions:
  a. How many grams of protein are contained in 100g of the quiche?
  b. How many grams of fat are contained in the quiche?
  c. How many grams of fibre are contained in the quiche?
  d. How many grams of sugars are in 100g of the quiche?

7 Give **two** reasons why it is important for consumers to know what additives have been included in a food product.

Activities

1 Below is a list of food products. Choose the most appropriate production method and give reasons for your answers.
  ● frozen pizzas
  ● flapjacks
  ● canned peas
  ● bread rolls
  ● low-fat spread
  ● wedding cake.

2 How would you package the above products? Give reasons for your answer.

Product evaluation

What is evaluation?

Evaluation is an ongoing process throughout the development and manufacture of a new food product. Evaluation allows judgments to be made about a product and thus enables improvements to be made at each stage. The criteria used in the evaluation are usually taken from the design brief, the design specification and the product specification.

Why is evaluation important?

Evaluation is important for the following reasons …

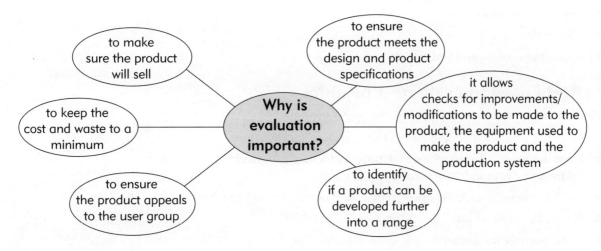

Figure 30: *Why is evaluation important?*

When does evaluation take place?

Here are some occasions when evaluation will take place:

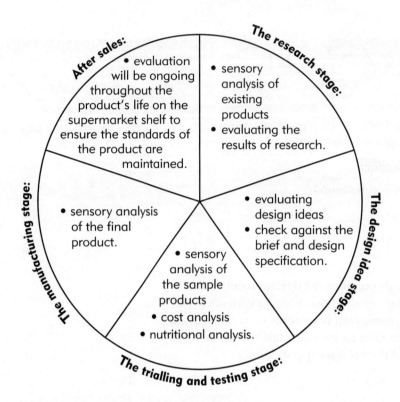

Figure 31: *Occasions for evaluation.*

Who carries out the evaluation?

- The user group
- The food manufacturer
- The retailer
- Magazines – consumer test articles.

Criteria used to evaluate a product

The following criteria can be used to evaluate a product:

- Does the product meet the design brief/product specification?
- Have the issues affecting the development of a new product been addressed e.g. moral, environmental, cultural?
- Are the costs of ingredients/production methods/packaging suitable?
- Is the new product value for money?
- Is the portion size correct?
- Are the taste, texture, appearance and aroma correct?
- Does the product meet the nutritional needs of the target group?
- Is the product environmentally friendly? This includes packaging and sources of ingredients.

- How does the product compare with other products produced by competitors?
- Does the control system work?
- Is the product easy to package?
- Is the product easy to transport?
- Is the product suitable for manufacture?
- Does the product have a suitable shelf life?

How are the results of evaluation recorded?

Evaluation results can be recorded in a number of ways. Some examples would be:

- tables
- star profiles/radar graphs
- reports.

Key points

- Evaluation is an ongoing process throughout the development and manufacture of a new product.
- Evaluation enables products to be improved.
- Evaluation should be against the design brief and design and product specification.

Questions

1 During the development of a new product it is necessary to evaluate the success of the product against the design and product specifications. Give **two** reasons why evaluation is an important part of product development.

2 State **two** stages in the development of a new product when evaluation would take place.

3 State **three** evaluation criteria a food manufacturer might use to judge a product.

Knowledge and Understanding

Materials and pre-manufactured standard components

This section will cover:

- Nutrients found in food.
- Functions of ingredients.
- Smart/modern foods.
- Food components.
- Food choice.
- Special dietary needs.

Nutrients found in food

When designing new food products, the nutrients contained in the product may form part of the specification. For example, to design and make a high protein, high iron cook-chill product for a lacto-vegetarian you would need to consider the following:

There are five main nutrient groups:

- proteins
- carbohydrates
- fats
- vitamins
- minerals.

All foods contain a mix of nutrients. Some foods are higher in some nutrients than others.

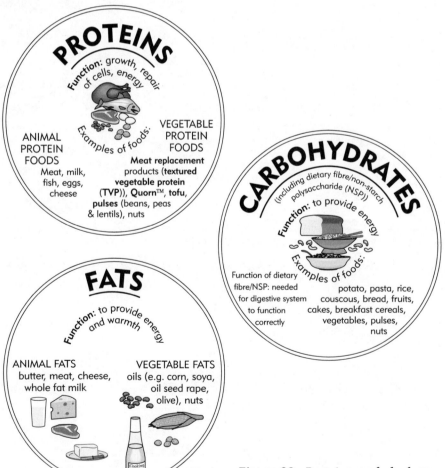

Figure 32: Proteins, carbohydrates and fats – the main points.

Key word

Meat analogues are also known as **meat replacements** and meat alternatives. Examples include TVP, Quorn™ and Tofu.

Pulses include peas, beans and lentils.

Textured vegetable protein or **TVP** is made from soya bean flour with the fat removed. TVP can be used to make burgers, sausages and ready-meals.

Quorn™ is an edible fungi. It is mixed with vegetable-based flavourings, rolled into sheets and then set by steaming. It can then be minced, cut into chunks, diced and made into products such as stir-fries and pies.

Tofu is a firm curd which can be used to make products such as burgers, ready meals and sausages. It is made by curdling soya milk with calcium sulphate.

Vitamins

Vitamin	Why needed?	Food sources
A	Eyesight, helps bones grow.	Carrots, apricots, eggs, tomatoes.
B complex	Helps release energy from foods.	Cereals, meat, fish, eggs, pulses.
C	Protects against infection, helps absorb calcium and iron.	Kiwi fruit, oranges, tomatoes, green vegetables.
D	Helps to absorb calcium to ensure healthy bones and teeth.	Oily fish e.g. mackerel, eggs, margarine.

Minerals

Mineral	Why needed?	Foods
Calcium	Strengthens bones & teeth, correct working of nerves and muscles.	Milk, cheese, bones of canned fish e.g. sardines, green vegetables.
Iron	To make red blood cells (**haemoglobin**).	Liver, cocoa, watercress, dried fruit and pulses.

> **Key word**
>
> **Haemoglobin** is the oxygen-carrying protein in red blood cells.

Most food manufacturers will include the nutritional value of a product on the package.

NUTRITION		
TYPICAL COMPOSITION	Each Tart (82 g) provides	100 g (3½ oz) provide
Energy	895kJ/214kcal	1092kJ/261kcal
Protein	5.1 g	6.2 g
Carbohydrate	25.8 g	31.5 g
of which sugars	9.8 g	11.9 g
Fat	10.0 g	12.2 g
of which saturates	4.7 g	5.7 g
mono-unsaturates	4.2 g	5.1 g
polyunsaturates	1.1 g	1.4 g
Fibre	0.9 g	1.1 g
Sodium	0.2 g	0.2 g
This Pack contains 2 custard tarts		
INFORMATION		

Figure 33: Nutrition information.

Why might a consumer need to know the nutritional value of a product?

- Comparisons of the nutritional content of different products can be made.

- They may be on a special diet e.g. low fat/high fibre.

- It allows an informed choice to be made.

- To ensure they have a variety of nutrients/balanced diet.

- It may help them to decide what to serve with a product. For example, a product may be low in fibre therefore fibre-rich foods need to be added to a meal.

Functions of ingredients

When food products are designed, the ingredients are chosen because of what they do (their function). All ingredients have a function in a food product. Here is a list of functions and examples of foods which are used to fulfil that function:

Functions	Example
Coating	Chocolate is used to coat biscuits.
Glazing	Egg glaze on the top of bread products.
Aerating	Eggs used in a whisked sponge.
Binding ingredients together	Milk used to bind a scone mixture together.
Bulking	Flour used in pastry and bread.
Setting	Gelatine used to set a jelly.
Thickening	Flour used to thicken a white sauce.
Adding flavour	Herbs and spices add flavour to a variety of food products.
Adding texture	Nuts can add texture to cakes.
Emulsifying	Egg yolks added to mayonnaise.
Preserving	Vinegar is used to preserve onions.
Shortening	Lard or white vegetable fat will give pastry a crisp and crumbly texture.
Sweetening	Honey is added to cakes.
Adding moisture	Milk is added to a batter.

Key word

Aerating – foods are made lighter by adding air or other gases.

Key words

Emulsifying stops ingredients separating out. For example, egg yolks added to mayonnaise prevent oil and vinegar separating out.

Preserving – to make food last longer.

Shortening adds texture to a product, giving a crumbly texture without adding flavour to a food product.

Smart/modern foods

Smart food (sometimes known as modern or novel food) is a collective term for newly developed food materials.

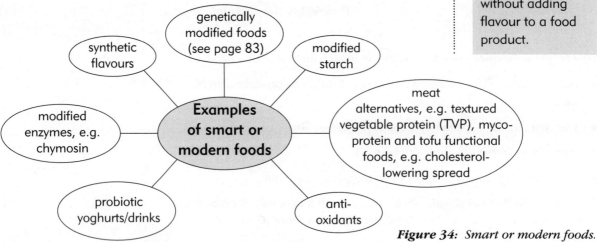

Figure 34: Smart or modern foods.

What is a smart or modern food?

Smart or modern foods are foods which will respond to differences in temperature or light and change in some way. These changes do not occur naturally but have been brought about through the invention of new or improved processes.

Let us look at one of these examples in greater detail:

Modified starch

This is a starch that has been altered (or modified) to perform additional functions.

Below are some examples of how modified starch is used in food products.

- Pre-gelatinised starch is used to thicken instant desserts without heat. Cold liquid such as milk can be added and the dessert will thicken.
- Cheese sauce granules or gravy granules – boiling water can be added to thicken without the product going lumpy.
- Commercial pizza toppings often contain modified starch. The topping thickens when heated in the oven so that it stays on top of the pizza and then becomes runny when it cools.
- Modified starch is used as a fat replacement in low-fat meals.
- Modified starch is added to prevent 'drip' after a product is defrosted.
- It is used in sauces, for example, in lasagne or macaroni cheese.
- The noodles in 'pot snacks' are pre-gelatinised, so boiled water will re-heat and 'cook' them.
- Modified starch is used in 'cup-a-soups' to improve mouth-feel, thicken the drink with the addition of boiled water, and blend uniformly with no lumps.

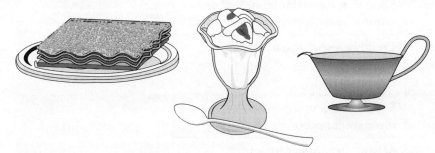

Figure 35: Uses of modified starch.

Food components

The word 'component' is used to describe an individual part that makes up a product. For example, flour is a component of pastry, and pastry is a component of a sausage roll.

Often food manufacturers will buy in **pre-manufactured standard components**. For example, a food manufacturer or food retailer producing pizzas may buy in the ready-made pizza bases, tomato topping, grated cheese and chopped vegetables.

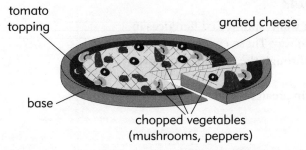

Figure 36: *The pre-manufactured standard components used in the manufacture of a pizza.*

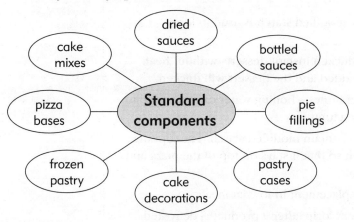

Figure 37: *Examples of pre-manufactured standard components.*

What are the benefits and limitations of using pre-manufactured standard components in the food industry?

Benefits	Limitations
May be cheaper than producing their own.	Special storage conditions may be required e.g. freezers, refrigerators.
They may not have the facilities/equipment to produce their own.	Could be expensive to buy in.
Maintain consistency of end product.	Supplier may produce an inconsistent product.
Saves time by reducing number of manufacturing processes.	Reliant on supplier to deliver on time.
Reduce costs, as little or no skill is required to use them.	Reliant on supplier to produce a product that meets hygiene regulations.
Keeps the assembly process as simple as possible.	
Maintain stock control – some components have a relatively long shelf life.	

Food choice

A food manufacturer needs to have an understanding of what affects the consumer's choice of food.

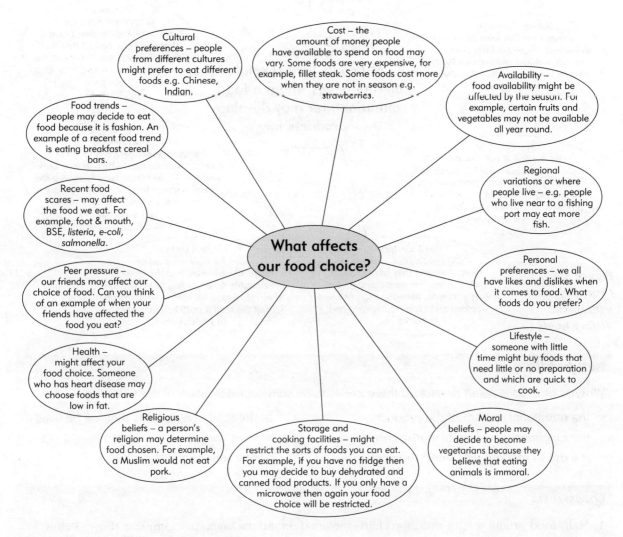

Figure 38: *What affects our choice of food?*

Special dietary needs

Many people have special dietary needs. Often a food manufacturer will develop food products specifically aimed at groups of people with special dietary needs.

Other people who have special dietary requirements include pregnant women, the elderly and convalescents. However, food manufacturers do not specifically design food products for these groups of people.

Children – many products are developed and aimed at children. For example, the Sainsbury's 'Blue Parrot' range. The size of the portions, the nutritional and additive content have all been considered.

Lacto vegetarians – people who do not eat meat or fish but will eat dairy products such as milk, cheese, yoghurt and butter.

Vegans – people who will not eat any animal products.

Babies – products aimed at babies have been developed. These products contain no salt or sugar and are usually smooth in texture so that they can be easily digested.

Groups of people with special dietary needs whom a food manufacturer may develop products for

Diabetics – people who have too much glucose in their blood-stream due to the fact that their bodies are not able to convert the glucose from food into energy.

Overweight or obese – one of the reasons people become overweight or obese is because they eat too many food products that are high in fat and sugar. Food products are developed which are low in fat and sugar.

Coeliacs – people who are sensitive to the protein gluten, which is found in products made from wheat, barley, oats and rye. These people have to have a diet which is gluten free. Gluten free products are clearly labelled with a symbol. (see page 48).

Figure 39: Groups of people with special dietary needs.

Food allergies – many people have allergies to foods therefore they have to avoid eating them. The most common are allergies to milk, peanuts, eggs, fish and seafood and certain colourings and preservatives.

Religious groups – food for Muslims must be halal, which means that the animals are slaughtered according to Muslim law. Jewish food must be kosher, which means that the food is prepared according to Jewish laws.

Key points

When a product is being developed there needs to be some consideration of the following:

- the nutritional content of the product
- the functions of individual ingredients
- the use of modern and smart materials
- the food components that will be used
- food choice
- any special dietary needs.

Questions

1 Many food products have nutrition charts included on the package. An example is shown below:

NUTRITION

Typical values	Per 100 g
Energy	**302 kcal**
Protein	4 g
Carbohydrates	65.4 g
of which sugars	32.8 g
Fat	4.4 g
of which saturates	1.7 g
Fibre	0.7 g
Sodium	0.4 g

Give **two** benefits to consumers of having a nutrition chart on the package of a food product.

2 Name **two** meat replacement products that could be used in burgers and pies.

3 When developing products it is important to know the functions of ingredients. Complete the following table by adding **two** examples of foods which can perform each of the listed functions. The first one is completed for you.

Function	Example 1	Example 2
Glazing	Egg	Milk
Sweeten		
Bulking		
Thickening		
Aerating		
Binding		
Setting		
Preserving		
Emulsifying		

4 All ingredients have a function. Complete each of the following sentences:

Honey is used as a glaze on ....

Dried fruits are used to sweeten ....

Bread is used as bulk in ....

Rice is used as bulk in ....

Yeast is used to aerate ....

Egg is used to bind ....

Egg is used to set ....

Sugar is used to preserve ....

5 Below is a table of ingredients for cheese and onion scones. State **one** function of each of the ingredients listed.

Ingredient	Function
200g self raising flour	
50g hard margarine	
Pinch of salt	
50ml milk	
50g mature Cheddar cheese	

6 Below is a list of standard components used in the food industry. Name **three** products that could be made using each of the components. An example has been completed for you.

Example: Frozen pastry – fruit pie, savoury flan, sausage rolls.

Grated cheese ....

Pie fillings ....

Jam ....

Custard ....

7 Give **two** reasons why consumers may prefer to eat food that does not contain animal products.

Activities

1 What ready-made components have you used when carrying out practical work? What were the reasons for using these?

2 Give an example of a pre-manufactured standard component. What are the limitations/benefits for the food manufacturer when using this component?

3 Carry out some research to find out about the following 'smart foods':
  ● probiotic yoghurts
  ● genetically modified foods
  ● cholesterol-lowering spreads
  ● meat alternatives.

4 Think of a suitable meal for the following group of people and give reasons for your choice:
  ● lacto vegetarians
  ● vegans
  ● coeliacs.

Systems and control

What is a system?

A system is a collection of elements which work together to perform a task. Before a new food product can be produced, systems need to be in place. A food production system is a group of events that work together to manufacture food products. These systems will enable products to be made:

- safely
- hygienically
- cost-effectively
- efficiently
- consistently
- to an expected quality.

Control systems used in the food industry

Systems are put in place in the food industry to control the production of food products.

A system has three parts:

INPUT – starts up a system	The input consists of materials, ingredients, components and/or energy. These are put into the system.
PROCESS – the way the system changes	The process consists of the manufacturing processes and activities which turn the input into an output.
OUTPUT – the end result	The output is the finished product and any waste products that can be sold as a by-product.

A recipe is an example of a system. It has an input (the ingredients), a process (the method) and an output (the finished product).

As an example, let's make a cheese and pickle sandwich …

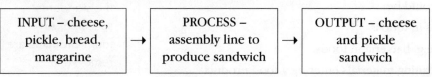

INPUT – cheese, pickle, bread, margarine → PROCESS – assembly line to produce sandwich → OUTPUT – cheese and pickle sandwich

There is also a fourth element in a system, which is called **feedback**. Feedback is used to control a system. The feedback on the sandwich may come from carrying out sensory analysis on the sandwich and might state, for example, that there is too much pickle and not enough cheese.

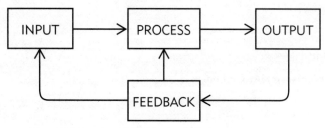

Figure 40: *Information is fed back to ensure all parts of the system are working correctly.*

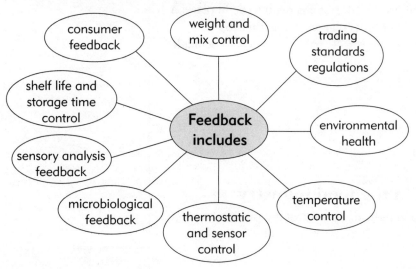

Figure 41: *Elements of feedback.*

Potential hazards and how to control them using HACCP charts

The Food Safety Act (1995) requires all **food premises** to assess the potential **hazards** and to take the required action to ensure the safety of food. These potential hazards are identified using a system known as HACCP (**H**azard **A**nalysis and **C**ritical **C**ontrol **P**oint). HACCP is carried out by **quality assurance** managers. The potential hazards are identified and **quality control** measures are put in place to minimise the hazard.

What hazards might be identified in the manufacture of a product?

Some examples of hazards could be:

- Physical hazards e.g. glass in foods.
- Microbiological hazards e.g. bacteria in foods.
- Chemical hazards e.g. cleaning materials entering a food product.

For every food product that is manufactured a HACCP chart is drawn up. Below is an example of a HACCP system for making an egg sandwich.

	Process	Hazard	Risk level of hazard	Control measures	Critical control point?	Tests for control
1	Collect eggs	Eggs may contain *Salmonella*.	High risk.	Store eggs away from other ingredients. Reject cracked eggs.	Yes	Check refrigerator temperature is at or below 5°C. Handle eggs with care.
2	Collect sandwich ingredients	Ingredients may not be safe to eat.	Medium risk.	Keep chilled foods cold. Check datemark of ingredients and quality.	No	Check refrigerator temperature is at or below 5°C.
3	Boil the egg until hard, then cool in cold water	Eggs may contain *Salmonella*. Egg shells can cause physical contamination of sandwiches.	High risk.	Make sure the egg is boiled for 10 minutes.	Yes	Cook the egg for the correct temperature and time.
4	Mash the egg with bottled mayonnaise for the filling.	Eggs and mayonnaise are high-risk foods.	High risk.	Mix quickly and store for a short time in cool conditions.	Yes	Check refrigerator temperature is at or below 5°C. Store for a limited time.
5	Make the sandwiches	Food handlers may not work hygienically.	High risk.	Train food handlers in good hygiene practices and make and store the sandwiches quickly.	Yes	Check food handlers for hygiene and safety. Keep preparation area cool and clean.
6	Store sandwiches for eating	Bacteria can multiply in warm temperatures and over time.	High risk.	Check that sandwiches are cool, clean and covered.	Yes	Store in refrigerator at or below 5°C for less than 4 hours.

Figure 42: A HACCP chart.

What needs to be controlled?

Food manufacturers and retailers need to make sure that all necessary controls are put in place. A food manufacturer or retailer needs to ensure that …

- food is bought from reputable suppliers
- food is stored at the correct temperature
- raw and cooked foods are kept separate at all times
- chilling and freezing of food is at the correct temperature
- food is cooked at the correct temperature for correct length of time
- correct cleaning procedures of equipment and premises are put in place
- correct pest control is in place
- metal detection is in place
- machinery is working correctly

- staff are trained in food hygiene
- stock is rotated
- hot food is kept at the correct temperature
- the weight of a product is accurate
- the size and shape of a product is consistent.

How are temperature and weight controlled?

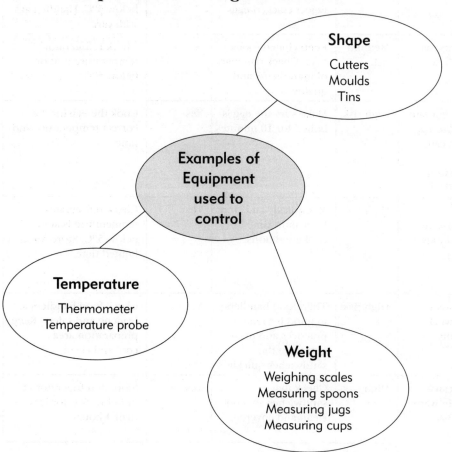

Figure 43: *Examples of equipment used to control temperature, weight and shape.*

Key points

- A system is a collection of elements, which work together to perform a task.
- Systems enable products to be made: safely, hygienically, cost-effectively, efficiently, consistently, to an expected quality.
- Systems are put in place in the food industry to control the production of food products.
- A system has three main parts: *input*, *process* and *output*
- There is also a fourth element in a system, which is called feedback.
- Potential hazards are identified using a system known as HACCP.
- Food manufacturers and retailers need to make sure that all necessary controls are put in place. These controls include temperature and weight controls.

Questions

1 What does HACCP stand for?

2 List **three** controls which a food manufacturer needs to put in place.

3 Define and explain the term 'quality assurance'.

4 Define and explain the term 'quality control'.

5 Feedback is an important element in a system. Explain what is meant by the term feedback.

Activities

1 Produce a simple HACCP plan for a recipe you have tried out. Write your HACCP plan in a table using the following headings.

Hazard	Method	Control

2 In your own words explain what the three stages of a system involve. Apply this to the making of a ham, lettuce and tomato sandwich.

Products and applications

What is product analysis and when would it be carried out?

Product analysis consists of looking at all aspects of a product in detail. One of the responsibilities of the product development team is to carry out product analysis of existing products.

The product development team will carry out product analysis on competitors' products as well as their own. They would carry out the product analysis at the research stage. (See page 13.)

The product development team may carry out product analysis on one product or several. For example, a food manufacturer may have a brief from a retailer to develop a new chilled dessert. Therefore the product development team would buy a range of chilled desserts from a number of supermarkets as part of their research.

The product development team will analyse both the food and the packaging.

Why carry out product analysis?

Product analysis is done in order to:

- investigate how a product is made
- analyse the types and amounts of ingredients used
- gain ideas for new product development
- compare differences between brands
- check that a product matches its specification.

Considerations when carrying out product analysis

Here are a list of questions a product development team might ask when they are carrying out product analysis.

- **Target market.** Who is the product aimed at and why?
- **Purpose of the product.** What is the purpose of the product? How and when would the product be used?

- What ingredients and additives have been used and what are their functions?
- What manufacturing processes have been used? For example, has the product been blast-chilled, dehydrated, blast-frozen?

Testing the product

This will involve sensory analysis. Sensory analysis involves looking at appearance, taste, texture, aroma (see page 21). Testing involves looking at the following issues:

Disassemble the product – It might be necessary to check any claims that are being made about the product. For example, if a food manufacturer claims that a product contains 70% meat, then the product could be disassembled to check that this claim is accurate.

Analyse packaging – What materials have been used for packaging and why?

Value – What is the cost of the product? Is the product good value for money compared to similar products?

Promotion – How is the product promoted? How does the product attract the consumer? Is the packaging attractive? Does the product make special claims, for example 'low in fat'? What alternative products are available and what makes this product more attractive?

Environment – Has the manufacturer considered environmental issues when developing the product? For example, is the packaging material used recyclable? Are organic ingredients added?

Health and safety – Have there been any safety considerations when developing the product? For example, tamper-proof packaging. Are the serving suggestions suitable?

Weight and size – Is the portion size suitable for the number of people the product claims to serve? Are the weight claims correct?

Alternative products – What alternative products are available and what makes this product attractive to consumers?

EXAMPLE OF PRODUCT ANALYSIS

Functions of ingredients

Ingredient	Function
Dried pasta (66%)	Bulk
Tomato powder (12%)	Flavour
Sugar	Flavour
Modified potato starch	Instant thickener for instant viscosity
Hydrogenated vegetable oil	Texture and flavour
Glucose syrup	Bulking agent, texture
Salt	Flavour
Yeast extract	Flavour
Onion powder	Flavour
Milk protein	Texture, gives a creamy flavour, colour
Acidity regulator (Dipotassium Phosphate)	Flavour, reduces the acidity of the product
Dried herbs	Flavour
Colour (paprika extract)	Colour
Flavourings	Flavour
Citric acid	Regulates the pH of the product

Target groups –
older teenagers, adults, possibly people on a diet, possibly vegetarians, elderly.

Purpose of the product –
to provide a quick hot snack which needs little preparation and no cooking. Could be eaten at school, at work or at home. The product is cheap, nutritious, light to carry home from the shop, has a long shelf life.

Promotion of product
The packaging is brightly coloured. It is mainly red which reflects the tomato flavour and the red colour of the product. The product has simple pictorial instructions for making.

Processing methods used
Dry blend of powders with added dried pasta.

Packaging materials
Barrier-coated laminate paper pouch with a foil lining to prevent moisture transfer and maximise shelf life.

Safety points
The manufacturer has pointed out that the product has been produced in a factory that handles nuts.

Results of disassembling the product
The product in total weighed 64g with 44g (66%) of dried pasta.

Cost
44p. This is slightly cheaper than other brand dehydrated snacks.

Summary of sensory analysis
Good tomato flavour, flavour of herbs is not very strong probably due to the very strong tomato flavour.
Lots of pasta, rather too much, good consistency for a snack product. Colour looks slightly too red and artificial. Aroma has quite a strong onion smell. The texture of the pasta is a little too soft.

Figure 44: Analysis of a product.

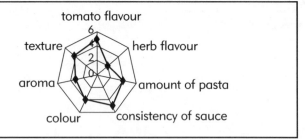

Figure 45: Star graph showing sensory analysis results.

Key points

- Product analysis is looking at all aspects of a product in detail.
- The product development team carry out product analysis on existing products.
- Product analysis is carried out to:
  - investigate how a product is made
  - analyse the types and amounts of ingredients used
  - gain ideas for new product development
  - compare differences between brands
  - check that a product matches its specification.

Activity

Now it's your turn to carry out product analysis. Find a commercially manufactured food product and use the table below to aid your analysis.

Name of Product ....

User group	
Purpose of product	
Ingredients and functions	
Manufacturing processes	
Sensory analysis	
Disassemble	
Materials used for packaging	
Cost of the product	
Promotion	
Environment issues	
Safety issues	
Size of product	
Alternative products	

Quality

This section will cover:

- Quality assurance and quality control procedures.
- Shelf life of food products, including:
  - food storage
  - food spoilage
  - food poisoning.

Quality assurance and quality control procedures

To obtain a quality product that is safe to eat there need to be checks made throughout the manufacturing and retailing processes. Two systems are set up in the food industry to ensure a quality product that is safe.

What is quality assurance?

This is a system which is in place throughout the whole process of designing and making a food product. It begins at the development stage and continues to the retailing stage. It is a system that identifies any problems that are likely to occur and sets up control systems to stop them from happening. This system is set up to guarantee that the food product being produced is of good quality and safe to eat.

Quality assurance checks might include:

- specification checks
- hygiene procedures
- monitoring waste
- sensory analysis.

What is quality control?

This is a system which is set up to check quality. Quality control is part of quality assurance.

Quality control checks might include:

- weight checks
- measurement checks
- temperature checks
- checks for foreign bodies e.g. by using metal detectors
- checks for bacteria.

Shelf life of food products

The length of time that a food product will last without deteriorating (going off) is known as the shelf life.

But how does the consumer know how long a product will keep for? All food products are date stamped by law.

Important note

ISO 9000 is a series of international standards for the management of quality assurance. It establishes organisational structures and processes for ensuring that food products meet a consistent and agreed level of quality for consumers. It gives greater efficiency in quality control systems.

The two types of date stamping which are required by law are the

- 'use by' date
- 'best before' date.

The 'use by' date is found on products that are **high risk** such as raw meat and fish. These are known as **perishable** foods. The 'use by' date indicates the last date on which the product can be eaten. The food product will have a date shown as the day and the month. After this date, although the food may look fine, it is unsafe to eat.

Figure 46: 'Use by' stamp.

The 'best before' date can be found on food products, which are **low risk**, for example, canned products, frozen products, **dehydrated** products. The date stamp shows the day, month and year.

Figure 47: 'Best before' stamp.

Although not required by law, an additional date stamp – 'display until' – is sometimes included in food packaging. This indicates to a food retailer when a food product should be removed from sale.

Food storage

Food must be stored correctly at all times to prevent spoilage.

The food manufacturer

The food manufacturer has to ensure that food is stored in the correct conditions at all stages of the manufacture of a food product, including:

- choosing and buying components
- transporting components to the factory
- storing components at the factory until they are needed
- preparing the components
- cooking the components
- storing food products once they have been manufactured
- transporting food products from the factory to the retailer.

The food retailer

Correct storage conditions must continue once a food product reaches the retailer.

Some products need to be kept at **ambient temperature** (room temperature), which is between 20°C and 25°C. These products include bread, flour, sugar and canned and dried food.

Supermarkets operate freezers at between −18°C and −20°C. Frozen products include vegetables, meat, desserts, bread and frozen ready meals.

Chilled products, such as cook-chill meals, dairy produce and fresh meat should be kept at a temperature of between 5°C and 8°C. Supermarkets also chill fresh fruit and vegetables.

Key words

High risk foods are foods which spoil in a short amount of time e.g. meat and fish.

Perishable foods are those which go off or spoil quickly.

Low risk foods are foods which have a long shelf life.

Dehydrated foods have had the moisture removed.

Key word

Ambient temperature is normal room temperature – between 20°C and 25°C

In the home

It is then the responsibility of the consumer to store the food in the correct conditions. The main food storage areas in the home are the fridge, freezer and cupboards. The temperature of a domestic refrigerator should be 5°C or below. The temperature of a domestic freezer should be −18°C or below.

The diagram below shows a fridge and indicates where foods should be stored.

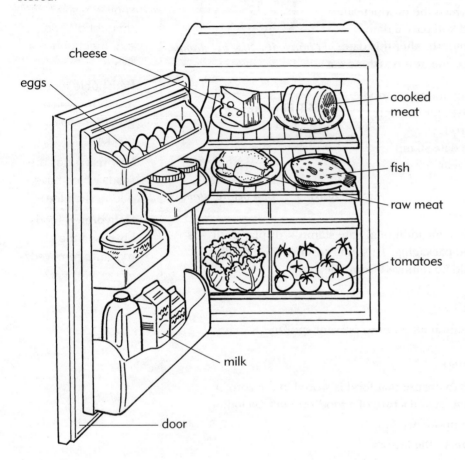

Figure 48: Fridge storage.

Manufacturers must always be clear on their packaging how foods should be stored in the home. The following are examples of storage information found on a variety of products:

| STORE IN A COOL DRY PLACE | – e.g. Tea, coffee, flour, stuffing mix.

| BEFORE OPENING STORE IN A COOL DRY PLACE
AFTER OPENING KEEP REFRIGERATED AND USE WITHIN 4 WEEKS |

– e.g. Tomato ketchup, mayonnaise, salad dressing.

| KEEP REFRIGERATED | – e.g. Cheese, margarine, eggs.

Food spoilage

There are two chief causes of food spoilage. These are micro-organisms (such as bacteria, yeasts and moulds) and enzymes.

Fact file on bacteria

Bacteria are found in soil, water, decaying food, and humans.

To grow, bacteria need food, moisture, warmth and time.

Most bacteria can survive and multiply within a very wide temperature range of between 5°C and 63°C. This is known as the DANGER ZONE.

Below 0°C bacteria will become dormant.

Most bacteria cannot survive at a temperature of 70°C or above.

Fact file on yeasts

Found in the air, skin of some fruits, and soil.

Do not need oxygen to reproduce.

Like warm, moist conditions.

Destroyed at temperatures of 100°C or above.

Will remain dormant in cold conditions.

Fact file on moulds

Visible to the eye.

Can affect the appearance and texture of food.

Usually found on the surface of food.

Fact file on enzymes

They are proteins.

Speed up chemical reactions.

Enzymes are found in all foods.

Useful micro-organisms

Not all micro-organisms are harmful. Micro-organisms are used in the production of the following products:

- bread (yeast)
- beer & wine (yeast)
- cheese (bacteria and enzymes)
- blue cheese (moulds)
- yoghurt (bacteria)
- Quorn™ (fungi).

Food poisoning

Most cases of food poisoning are caused by bacteria. The bacteria which are most likely to cause food poisoning are *Salmonella*, *Staphylococcus aureus*, *Campylobacter* and *Escherichia coli (E. coli)0157*.

Symptoms of food poisoning include fever, stomach cramps, vomiting, diarrhoea, and in some cases, death.

High risk foods

Some foods are more likely to cause food poisoning. These foods are called 'high risk foods'. Examples of high-risk foods include cooked and raw meat and poultry, shellfish, fish, cooked rice, eggs, soft cheese and milk.

These foods are more likely to cause food poisoning as they either have a high moisture content or are foods which are rich in protein.

How can food poisoning be prevented?

- Avoiding **cross contamination** between raw and cooked foods when preparing, and storing.
- Good personal hygiene e.g. washing hands after going to the toilet, sneezing or coughing and before and after handling food.

Key word

Cross contamination is the transfer of hazardous substances from one area to another. For example, bacteria from raw meat could be passed onto cooked meat if the same chopping board were used.

- Ensuring food is thrown away once the 'use by' date has passed.
- Storing food at the correct temperature.
- Ensuring food is defrosted thoroughly.
- Ensuring food is reheated thoroughly.

Why has there been an increase in food poisoning?

- More people are eating out.
- Increased use of microwaves often means foods are not defrosted or cooked for the correct length of time.
- Increased use of cook-chill and frozen products.
- Incorrect storage of food products.
- Incorrect preparation of foods e.g. foods not thawed for the correct amount of time or foods prepared too far in advance.
- Not reheating foods to correct temperature for the correct length of time.
- Inadequate hygiene training for people working with food.
- Hot foods kept hot below 63°C.

Important note

To avoid cross contamination, different coloured chopping boards and knives can be used.

Raw fish – blue.

Raw meat – red.

Fruit and vegetables – green.

Cooked meat – yellow.

Key points

- Quality assurance and quality control systems ensure that quality food products are available to consumers.
- The shelf life of a product is the length of time a product will last without deteriorating.
- 'Use by' and 'best before' dates inform the consumer if the food product is safe to eat and is of good quality.
- To maintain a good quality food product food must be stored correctly.
- Food spoilage will occur if food is not stored correctly or if it has reached the end of its shelf life.
- Food poisoning can result if food is not stored and cooked correctly.

Questions

1 A family go out for the day, and for lunch decide to take a picnic. Their picnic consists of ham sandwiches, cooked chicken legs, salad, a packet of crisps, a cream cake and a drink of orange juice. The next day they all develop food poisoning. Name **two** foods which could have caused the food poisoning.

2 Look at the list of ingredients below for fresh chicken and vegetable soup and identify **three** high risk ingredients.

   CHICKEN · SUNFLOWER OIL · ONION · LEEK · CARROTS · CELERY · GARLIC · FRESH STOCK · RICE · FRESH HERBS · SALT AND PEPPER

3 Where should raw meat be stored in the refrigerator? Give **one** reason for your answer.

4 How should tomato ketchup be stored once it has been opened?

5 Why should different coloured chopping boards be used when preparing foods?

6 What colour chopping board would you use for the following foods?
   - raw fish
   - raw meat
   - fruit and vegetables
   - cooked meat.

Health and safety

> **This section will cover:**
> - Food safety and the law
> - Environmental issues
> - Food issues.

Food safety and the law

What Acts protect the consumer?

There are many acts which protect the consumer and ensure food is safe to eat. Some examples include:

The Food Safety Act 1990
Introduced to ensure all food produced at any stage in the food industry, including food production, manufacture and retail, is safe to eat.

The Food Safety (General Food Hygiene) Regulations 1995
This act gives instructions about food hygiene standards in the food industry

The Food Safety (Temperature Control) Regulations 1995
This act requires high risk foods to be kept at below 8°C, and cooked or reheated food that should be served hot, at 63°C.

The Food Labelling Regulations 1999
This describes the information that must be on a food label. (See page 46.)

Who protects the consumer?

Trading standards officers and environmental health officers are responsible for protecting the consumer and enforcing the acts where necessary. A short summary of their jobs appears in the diagrams below.

Figure 49: *What does a trading standards officer do?*

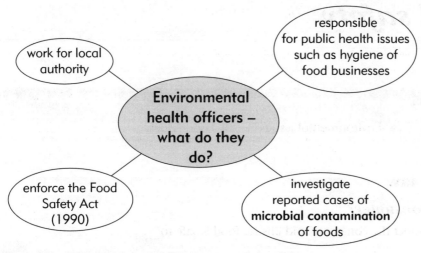

Figure 50: What do environmental health officers do?

Environmental issues

When designing and making food products manufacturers need to consider environmental issues. These issues include:

- packaging
- use of chemicals in the manufacturing process
- disposal of waste products.

Packaging

Why is packaging an environmental issue?

- Natural resources are used, for example, trees, metals & oil.
- It is not always easy to dispose of and can therefore cause pollution of the environment.

Food manufacturers can address this problem by doing the following:

- using materials that the consumer can **recycle**
- using materials that are **biodegradable**
- reducing the amount of packaging
- avoiding harmful processes when producing packaging, for example, bleaching wood pulp
- encouraging consumers to consider recycling or disposing of packaging in an environmentally safe way, by including one of the following symbols.

Figure 51: Keep Britain tidy.

Figure 52: Recycle!

How can the consumer (you!) address the problem?

You have a responsibility to help address this problem too. There are many things you can do, amongst which are:

- reusing packaging e.g. jars, bottles, bags

- reusing carrier bags

- taking waste materials such as paper or glass to recycling centres

- buying products that have minimal packaging

- selecting biodegradable packages

- disposing of packaging in a considerate and sensible way.

Using chemicals in the manufacturing process

Manufacturers should avoid using processes which use harmful chemicals such as bleach and **CFCs**, so that they do not get released into water sources and the atmosphere.

Disposal of waste products

Manufacturers and retailers all have a duty to dispose of waste products safely. Waste will include food waste, processing waste (such as fat from deep fat frying) and packaging waste.

Food issues

Genetic modification of foods

The characteristics of foods can be altered by using genetic modification. Genetic modification involves identifying and altering a specific gene which has a specific function in a food product. The first genetically modified food product on sale in the UK was tomato purée made from tomatoes which ripen slowly. This allows the tomatoes to be left for longer before picking without going soft. It also allows greater time for processing before the food spoils thus saving money.

Crops have also been developed that are resistant to pests and disease. The advantages of this are that fewer pesticides need to be used on crops.

There has been much controversy about the safety of developing genetically modified foods. Some groups of people are concerned that modified genes might be transferred from one species to another.

Organic foods

Organic foods are foods that have been grown without the aid of artificial chemicals and are becoming increasingly popular among consumers. The cost of organic foods is often higher than that of non-organic alternatives.

All food sold as organic must come from growers, processors or importers who are registered and subject to regular inspection.

Other recent food issues include the use of food additives, BSE and CJD (the human form of BSE) and foot and mouth disease.

> ### *Key word*
>
> **CFCs** – Chlorofluorocarbon (CFC) is a chemical released into the atmosphere through the use of refrigerators and aerosols. It is considered harmful to the ozone layer.

Key points

Health and Safety is an important issue for the manufacturer, retailer and consumer.

- The consumer is protected by:
  - food acts and regulations
  - trading standards officers
  - environmental health officers.
- A number of environmental issues should be considered by the manufacturer, retailer and consumer.
- There are a variety of food issues which will affect the development of a new food product as well as consumer choice.

Questions

1 Give **three** responsibilities of a trading standards officer.

2 List **two** ways in which you the consumer can help the environment when buying food products.

3 What are the benefits of buying food products made with organic ingredients?

Activities

1 List **three** food products. Describe how they are packaged and think about how that packaging could be reduced or be made more environmentally friendly.

2 Did you consider environmental issues when you developed a new food product for the GCSE coursework? If you did, what issues did you consider and make a list of these. If you didn't think about these issues, think about them now. Explain how you would ensure your product is environmentally friendly.

Specimen questions

The following pages show specimen questions and a mark scheme for the Food Technology examinations. Study each of the questions carefully, taking note of the marks available, and then use the mark scheme to see how you would have scored in an exam.

- The written exam is worth 40% of the total marks awarded. Remember your coursework is worth 60%.

- You will take **two** examination papers if you are entered for the full course.

- You will only take **one** examination paper if you are entered for the short course.

- Foundation candidates taking the full course will have **two** papers each **1 hour** in length (papers 1 and 3).

- Higher candidates taking the full course will have two papers each **1 hour 15 minutes** in length (papers 2 and 4).

- If you are entered for the foundation papers you can achieve between C to G grade.

- If you are entered for the higher papers you can achieve between A* to D grade.

- Each paper has **five** questions each worth 10 marks.

- The questions require you to write your answers in the appropriate space. At times you will also be required to sketch and annotate.

- On the first paper, question five will be a product analysis question.

- On the second paper, question three will be a product analysis question based upon a theme. This theme will be given to you a few weeks before the examination.

- The marks available are included in brackets after each part of a question.

Foundation paper

1 Sample question

1 A food manufacturer is developing a cook-chill lasagne.

(a) On the drawing of the product sleeve below, label the information shown. (3)

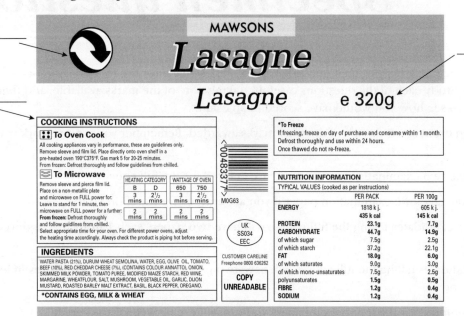

(b) The main ingredient in the lasagne filling is meat. Suggest two other ingredients which could be added to the filling to add colour and flavour.

Colour .... (1)

Flavour .... (1)

(c) Where are cook-chill products stored in a supermarket?

.... (1)

(d) At what temperature, by law, should cook-chill products be stored in a supermarket?

.... (1)

(e) Food manufacturers use colour-coded equipment for the preparation of food.
What is the recommended colour of a chopping board for the following foods? (3)

Food	Colour
Raw meat	
Vegetables	
Cooked meat	

Mark scheme

Question	Answer	Total marks available
1 (a)	One mark for each piece of information that is correctly labelled: recycling cooking instructions weight.	3 × 1
(b)	One mark for a food that adds colour, one mark for a food that adds flavour. Examples: Colour: (one from) carrots, peppers, sweetcorn, peas, spinach. Flavour: (one from) mushroom, herbs, peppers, leeks. Or any other foods which would add colour or flavour.	2 × 1
(c)	Storage in fridge	1
(d)	0–5°C or below 8°C	1
(e)	One mark for each correct answer: Raw meat – red Vegetables – green Cooked meat – yellow	3 × 1
		Total 10

2 Sample question

A food retailer wants to increase its range of summer desserts aimed at 5–10 year olds.

(a) What type of research might the food retailer carry out before developing the new dessert?

....

.... (2)

(b) Why is it important to carry out research?

.... (1)

(c) List **three** methods which the food retailer might use to promote the new range of desserts.

1 ....

2 ....

3 .... (3)

(d) Below are the specification points for a new cold dessert.

- appeal to 5–10 year olds
- include fruit
- layered
- cold.

Using the above specification points sketch and label your idea for a new dessert in the box below.

(2)

(e) State **two** reasons why your new product meets the specification points.

1 ....

2 .... (2)

Mark scheme

Question	Answer	Total marks available
2 (a)	Two from: surveys/questionnaires looking at/carrying out sensory analysis of existing products Internet/computer research looking in books/recipe books.	2 × 1
(b)	To find out if there is a need for a particular product	1
(c)	Three from: newspapers/magazines radio/TV leaflets free samples in-store tasting in-store promotion.	3 × 1
(d)	1 mark for a clear sketch 1 mark for labelling	2 × 1
(e)	Two from: (marks given for explanation only) ● Cold – explanation of how the dessert is cold. ● Suitable for age group – use of ingredients which would appeal, finish of product. ● Fruit – explanation of how fruit has been used. ● Layered – explanation of how the dessert has been layered.	2 × 1
		Total 10

3 Sample question

A small bakery has decided to produce character-shaped biscuits

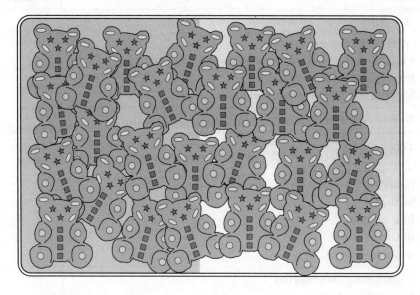

(a) Suggest **one** user group that this product is aimed at and give a reason for your answer.

User group ....

Reason .... (2)

(b) Name **two** methods that could be used to shape these biscuits.

1 ....

2 .... (2)

(c) (i) Name **one** method of production suitable for the manufacture of the shaped biscuits.

.... (1)

(ii) State **two** benefits of the named method of production.

Benefits	
1	
2	

(2)

(d) Give **three** reasons why people buy ready-made products.

1 ....

....

2 ....

....

3 ....

.... (3)

Mark scheme

Question	Answer	Total marks available
3 (a)	(One mark can be given for user group even if reason is incorrect.) Target group: young children Reason: the development of this biscuit designed to appeal to young children by using a shape that will attract them. • amusing shape • colourful • has sweets added.	2 × 1
(b)	Two from: • cutters • templates • moulds • rollers with blades.	2 × 1
(c) (i)	Batch production	1
(ii)	Two from: • A manufacturer can make small numbers and change the recipe each time. • Machinery can be used for other products. • Raw materials/components can be bought in bulk. • Cheaper than 'one-off' or 'job production'. Production costs are reduced as more products can be produced at the same time. • Only a small number of people are involved.	2 × 1
(d)	Three from: • saves time • quick to cook • easy to prepare • no preparation of raw ingredients needed • can be stored for a long time reducing the need to shop regularly • no waste • allows people to eat a range of products even if they lack the necessary skills • can work out cheaper if individual ingredients need to be bought • can be cooked in a microwave • easy to store • wide variety • saves time on washing up • good in emergencies.	3 × 1
		Total 10

4 Sample question

A food manufacturer is developing a range of savoury flans. Below is a table of ingredients showing the basic recipe.

Pastry case	Filling
200g plain flour	250ml milk
100g fat	2 eggs
$\frac{1}{4}$ teaspoon salt	75g cheese
cold water to mix	50g chopped onion
	salt & pepper

(a) Explain **one** function of each ingredient during the preparation and cooking of the savoury flan.

Ingredient	Function
Fat	
Water	
Salt	
Eggs	

(4)

(b) The product development team would like to extend the range. Suggest **two** changes, with reasons, which could be made.

Change 1	Reason
Change 2	Reason

(4)

(c) Give **two** reasons why egg products are classified as high-risk foods.

....

.... (2)

Mark scheme

Question	Answer	Total marks available
4 (a)	One mark given for each correct function:	
	Fat – coats flour grains to stop gluten forming when water is added, to make sure pastry has a short crumbly texture.	1
	Water – binds rubbed in fat/flour mix together, allows pastry to be rolled out easily.	1
	Salt – helps to develop the flavour.	1
	Eggs – when heated sets the mixture.	1
(b)	Addition of ingredients: e.g. broccoli, spinach, sweetcorn, tomato, peppers, herbs, ham, combination of two cheeses, mushrooms etc.	2 × 1
	Acceptable reasons: improves flavour, improves colour/appearance, improves the texture, improves the nutritional value.	2 × 1
(c)	One mark for each reason:	2 × 1
	High in protein, therefore ideal for the growth of bacteria. High moisture content, therefore ideal for the growth of bacteria.	
		Total 10

5 Sample question

Cereal bars have increased in popularity.

(a) State the purpose of this product.

.... (1)

(b) (i) Give **two** reasons why this product might appeal to young children.

1 ....

2 .... (2)

(ii) Give **two** reasons why parents might buy this product for their children.

1 ....

2 .... (2)

(c) Below is the nutritional information from the cereal bar.

Nutritional Information per 100g	
Energy	1900kj/450kcal
Protein	8g
Carbohydrates of which sugars	67g 49g
Fat	17g
Fibre	1.5g
Sodium	0.3g

State **two** reasons why this product may be considered unhealthy.

1 ....

2 .... (2)

(d) Standard components have been used in the manufacture of the cereal bar.
State **three** benefits for a food manufacturer of using pre-manufactured standard components.

1 ....

2 ....

3 .... (3)

Mark scheme

Question	Answer	Total marks available
5 (a)	One from: • to provide a quick alternative to breakfast/snack • to provide an easy to eat alternative breakfast/snack • replacement for breakfast/a meal.	1
(b) (i)	Two from: • appealing packaging makes product interesting • child-friendly lettering • cartoon character used • contains chocolate • can be eaten in the hand/easy to eat • are familiar with Coco Pops as a breakfast cereal.	2 × 1
(ii)	Two from: • contains milk • added vitamins • can be added to a lunch box • a quick alternative to breakfast when in a hurry • trusted brand.	2 × 1
(c)	Two from: • high in sugar • contains fat • low in fibre.	2 × 1
(d)	Three from: • maintain consistency of end product • saves time by reducing number of manufacturing processes • reduces costs as little or no skill is required to use them • keeps the assembly process as simple as possible • maintain stock control – some components have a relatively long shelf life.	3 × 1
		Total 10

Higher paper

1 Sample question

Labelling on packaging informs the consumer about a product.

(a) Name **two** pieces of packaging information that must be included by law.

1 ....

2 .... (2)

(b) In what order are the ingredients listed on a food product?

.... (1)

(c) Give one reason why food manufacturers include nutritional labelling on packaging.

.... (1)

(d) Materials used for packaging food products need careful selection.
State **two** benefits of each of the packaging materials listed below.

Packaging material	Benefit 1	Benefit 2
Glass		
Plastics		
Metals		

(6)

Mark scheme

Question	Answer	Total marks available
1 (a)	One mark for each piece of information: Name of product, ingredients, net weight/volume of product, name and address of manufacturer, 'use by' or 'best before' date, shelf life, storage conditions or conditions of use.	2 × 1
(b)	Weight order. Highest quantity of ingredient first.	1
(c)	One mark for one reason: Consumers know which nutrients are in the product. Comparisons of nutrient content of one food can be made with other foods. Informed choices can be made. Foods with a specific nutrient content can be selected e.g. low in fat, high in fibre.	1
(d)	One mark for each benefit given from: Glass Benefits: see-through/transparent, can print straight onto glass, recyclable/reusable, strong, can be used in microwave, moulded into a variety of shapes, inexpensive/cheap to produce. Plastics Benefits: lightweight, can be recyclable, can print straight onto plastic therefore a label isn't necessary, can be used in microwave to reheat a product, inexpensive/cheap, can be used in freezer, can be transparent/see-through, can be moulded into different shapes, can be coloured. Metal Benefits: recyclable, lightweight, keep their shape, withstand high temperatures, available in different thicknesses, can be moulded into a variety of shapes.	2 × 1 2 × 1 2 × 1
		Total 10

2 Sample question

The information below shows the results from sensory analysis testing of a prototype snack bar aimed at primary school children.

	Taster 1	Taster 2	Taster 3	Taster 4
Satisfying	5	5	4	5
Golden colour	1	1	1	2
Crumbliness	5	4	4	3
Crispiness	4	5	4	4
Amount of dried fruits	2	1	2	1
Size	5	4	4	5
Sweetness	5	4	4	5
Regular shape	1	2	1	2

(5 – very good; 3 – okay; 1 – poor)

(a) From the results above identify **two** characteristics which need improving and **explain** how each could be achieved.

Characteristic ....

Explanation ....

....

Characteristic ....

Explanation ....

.... (2)

(b) State **two** points in the development of a new product when sensory analysis would be carried out.

....

.... (2)

(c) State **two** conditions under which sensory analysis should be carried out and give reasons.

Condition 1 ....

....

Reason ....

....

Condition 2 ....

....

Reason ....

.... (4)

(d) State **two** ways in which the results of sensory analysis can be recorded.

1 ....

2 .... (2)

Mark scheme

Question	Answer	Total marks available
2 (a)	Characteristic & explanation must match: Amount of dried fruits – increase the amount of dried fruits added to the product. Regular shape – use a more accurate cutter/ template, ensure mixture not too wet. Golden colour – bake for longer.	2×1
(b)	Two from: • Research stage – manufacturers can compare their own products with those of competitors. Manufacturers might also carry out sensory analysis on their own product range. • In the test kitchen – it allows changes to be made to products before they go into production. This could therefore save time and money as products are more likely to sell. • Trialling and testing – when a new product has been developed and the team of developers want the target market to ensure product is acceptable. • During production – samples are taken of products to maintain and check the product is meeting the specification. • Marketing – can be used by the manufacturer when demonstrating the product to buyers. • Can be carried out in a supermarket to encourage consumers to buy the new product.	2×1
(c)	One mark for each correct condition. One mark for each correct reason. Marks for conditions can be awarded without a correct explanation. Two from: • Clear and easy to understand record sheets, so people are clear about what to record. • Food should be coded so that tasters are not influenced by numbers and letters e.g. '1 = the best'. • The same conditions for each taster in terms of the amount of light and temperature so that a fair test is carried out in the tasting booth. • Tasters should be in individual tasting booths so that they are not influenced by others. • The product should be presented in exactly the same way to all the tasters, for example, same-sized portions, same colour plate so that a fair test is carried out. • One sample should be given at a time so that tasters do not become confused. • Plain biscuits or a drink of water should be given between each sample, so that previous flavours don't affect the next product tasted. • Products should be given to the tasters at the correct temperature, so that foods are being tasted as the manufacturer intended.	2×1 2×1
(d)	Two from: • star profile/radar graph • computer spread sheet/Excel • table.	2×1
		Total 10

3 Sample question

Modified starch is classified as a smart food and is used by food manufacturers in a variety of products.

(a) Explain the function of modified starch in food production.

....

....

....

....

....

.... (4)

(b) Explain the benefits to food manufacturers of using additives in food products.

....

....

....

.... (2)

(c) Explain the benefits to consumers of additives in food products.

....

....

....

.... (2)

(d) Explain limitations to the consumer of including additives to food products.

....

....

....

.... (2)

Mark scheme

Question	Answer	Total marks available
3 (a)	Modified starch is a starch that has been altered to perform additional functions. Four functions from: • Pizza topping – topping thickens when heated in the oven and will not run off the pizza. On cooling the topping becomes runny. • Pre-gelatinised starch is used to thicken instant desserts without heat. Cold liquid such as milk can be added and the dessert will thicken. • Cheese sauce granules /gravy granules – boiling water can be added to thicken without the product going lumpy. • Modified starch is used as a fat replacer in low-fat meals. • Modified starch is added to prevent 'drip' after a product is defrosted. Modified starch is used in the sauce, e.g. lasagne or macaroni cheese. • The noodles in 'pot snacks' are pre-gelatinised, so boiled water will re-heat and 'cook' them. • Modified starch is used in 'cup-a-soups' to improve mouth-feel, thicken the drink/sauce with the addition of boiled water, and blend uniformly with no lumps.	4×1
(b)	Two from: • keeps food safe for longer by protecting against the growth of micro-organisms • preserves food/gives a longer shelf life • add or enhance flavour • add texture • add colour/can restore colour lost during production • makes product look more appealing • wide range of products can be produced • to help maintain consistency in large-scale production.	2×1
(c)	Two from: • can increase nutritional value e.g. vitamins added • food lasts longer so don't need to go shopping as often • increased variety of foods available • makes food safe by protecting against the growth of micro-organisms.	2×1
(d)	Two from: • Consumers may not buy a product because it may have an additive they object to e.g. vegans oppose the use of cochineal. • In some people can cause allergic reactions/people may have an intolerance. • Can be used to disguise inferior ingredients. • Some colours and flavours may not be necessary.	2×1
		Total 10

Answers to questions

Page 12

1 Possible answers include:

- views of the group are considered
- dietary needs can be taken into account
- eating habits are considered
- cooking method preferred
- appropriate portion size
- packaging and marketing of the product is focused on the user group
- the cost is appropriate.

2 Possible answers include:

- by looking at what competitors are producing
- by looking at what products already exist in their own range and thinking how a new range could be developed
- looking at trends in the media, for example, what is the current trend amongst TV chefs?
- carrying out supermarket surveys
- consulting government research e.g. The 'Five a day' campaign
- reading newspaper and magazine articles
- surfing the Internet
- carrying out interviews and questionnaires.

3 Possible answers include:

- the product must be marketable
- the type of product to be developed
- the user group or intended target market
- the cost.

4 The user group or the intended target market – is the person or group of people who will use the product e.g. a single portion cook-chill product might be eaten by a single person living alone.

Page 15

1 The purpose of a product is the reason or reasons for the existence of a product.

2 Possible answers include:

- to find out the opinions of the user group / intended target market
- to find out about types of products which are already on the market
- to ensure time and money are not wasted on a product no one will want
- to find out market trends, including shopping and eating habits
- to find out how successfully a product is selling.

3 Possible answers include:

- looking at what competitors are producing
- looking at which products already exist in their own range and thinking how a range could be developed
- sensory analysis
- looking at trends in the media, for example, what is the current trend amongst TV chefs?
- carrying out supermarket surveys
- consulting government research e.g. The 'Five a day' campaign
- reading newspaper and magazine articles
- surfing the Internet
- carrying out interviews and questionnaires.

4 A design specification is important because

- it identifies the qualities/criteria that the product should meet
- it provides a checklist for evaluation throughout the development of a product.

Pages 18–19

1 The sketch should be clear and annotated with approximate size of cake. Show how you have included buttercream, icing and a sponge cake base.

The explanation should clearly state how the design specification has been met.

Example explanation: The base is made of sponge cake. On top of the base is a layer of buttercream. On top of the butter cream is a layer of apricot jam. On top of the jam is a sponge cake layer, which is topped with peach-coloured and flavoured fondant icing. The size of the cake, approximately 4cm × 4cm, is a suitable portion for one person.

2 Possible answers include:
- Add a finish to the product e.g. finely grated lemon zest
- Incorrect colour of finished pastry – cook pastry case longer/shorter
- Sauce too thick – needs more liquid adding
- Sauce too thin – needs more thickening agent adding
- Lemon flavour needs increasing – add more lemon zest.

3 Possible answers include:
- cornish pasty – pastry leaf, egg/milk glaze
- lasagne – sprinkled cheese, slice of tomato
- sponge cake – layer of icing, piped butter cream, sugar,
- trifle – piped cream, slices of fresh fruit, glacé cherries, 100's and 1000's.

4 Possible answers include:
- annotated sketches
- mood boards
- concept boards
- photographs
- making up sample recipes.

Page 27

1 Numbers and letters could influence the tasters' opinions about a product. For example 'A' or '1' could be thought to be the best product.

2 **Ranking tests** involve placing products in order. For example, the taster could be asked to place five different beef burgers in order of preference.

Rating tests involve giving foods a score on a 1 – 5 scale.

Triangle tests are used to see if a taster can tell the difference between food products. This test is used if a manufacturer has been asked to develop a similar product to a competitor's.

3 Fat content reduced:
- use lean bacon
- remove bacon
- use low fat cheese
- reduce the amount of cheese.

Fibre content increased:
- add more vegetables e.g. sweet corn, peas
- use whole-wheat pasta
- use fresh tomatoes.

4 Possible answers include:
- add colourful ingredients to the product e.g. sweet corn, peas, peppers
- add a finish e.g. sliced tomatoes, parsley, red cheese, wholemeal breadcrumbs.

5 Possible answers include:
- fried bacon – grilled
- fried sausages – grilled, baked, casseroled
- fried egg – boiled, poached, scrambled
- fried chicken – baked, casseroled
- roast potatoes – baked, boiled.

6 Possible answers include:
- remove the minced beef and add pulses (peas, beans, lentils) or minced Quorn™, or minced TVP.

7 Possible answers include:
- raw materials
- purchase of specialised machinery
- overheads (fuel, lighting, heating, cooling, equipment depreciation, salaries)
- advertising
- marketing
- profit
- packaging inner and outer
- distribution costs
- offers have to be taken into consideration, for example 'buy one get one free'
- testing research and development.

8 Possible answers include:
- use cooking onions instead of shallots
- use oil or margarine instead of butter
- use long grain/Patna rice
- use water from cooking water of vegetables instead of stock cube
- replace prawns with a cheaper protein food e.g. minced beef
- replace prawns with vegetables e.g. sweet corn, peas, mushrooms
- use Cheddar cheese.

Page 30

1 Terminator, decision and process.

2 Possible answers include:
- biscuit dough – once shapes have been cut out, excess dough is collected, re-rolled and used again
- chocolate used to coat biscuits and icings on cakes – excess is re-used
- cake crumbs from cooked cakes are added back to a raw cake mixture.

3 Recipes are trialled and tested on a small scale, using small amounts of ingredients. Once a product has been accepted for manufacture, the ingredients in a recipe have to be increased in the correct proportions ready for mass production.

Page 35

1 Possible answers include:
- Enrobing machine – biscuits sit on a wire mesh and pass through a curtain of chocolate. Excess chocolate flows though the mesh into a bath below. As the biscuits pass over this bath, the bottom of the biscuits are coated with chocolate.
- Moulds – moulds are coated with chocolate. The biscuit is placed into the mould. More chocolate is then deposited on top to fully coat the product. The mould is then cooled and the biscuit is released.

2 Possible answers include:
- Loss of some jobs – often people who do unskilled jobs.
- Highly trained computer operatives required.
- Smaller workforce due to CAD/CAM – only a few people needed to produce a large quantity of products.

3

Application	Product development kitchen	Mass production or food factory
weighing and measuring ingredients	digital scales	computer-controlled weighing or measured into hoppers
mixing the cake mixture	mixing in a bowl with a wooden spoon or electric food mixer or food processor	giant mixing systems used
placing cake mixture in tins	spoon	depositor
baking the cake	oven	computer-controlled travelling or tunnel ovens
cooling the cake	cooling tray	blast-chilled in cooling tunnels

4
- can easily be seen if they come off, as very few foods are blue in colour
- contain a metal strip so can be detected by the metal detector should plaster fall into food.

Page 40

1 Possible answers include:
- increases the shelf life of a product/makes a product last longer
- prevents micro-organisms from multiplying
- prevents the action of enzymes
- increases the range of foods available
- convenience, fewer trips to the shops.

2 Possible answers include:

Benefits:
- foods keep their flavour and colour
- little or no alteration to the nutritional content.

Limitations:
- more costly than simply drying foods
- foods can become brittle so need careful handling.

3 −18°C to −20°C.

4 Between 0°C to 8°C. Most supermarkets would operate fridges at between 0°C and 5°C.

5 Possible answers include:
- meat – canned, frozen, dehydrated, salted, smoked, AFD, MAP
- potatoes – canned, frozen, dehydrated, irradiation
- fish – canned, frozen, salted, smoked, pickled
- apples – canned, frozen, dehydrated, irradiation.

6 Possible answers include:
- no need to defrost
- you don't have to remember to remove from the freezer
- better flavour/tastes more like a home-cooked product
- often fewer additives are used
- quicker to cook/reheat
- minimal changes in the nutritional content.

7 Possible answers include:

- they may not be able to cook for themselves
- many are sold in single portions and so are suitable for elderly people living alone
- easy to cook
- little or no preparation
- saves buying individual ingredients.

Page 43

1 CAD – Computer Aided Design.
  CAM – Computer Aided Manufacture.

2 Possible answers include:

- desk-top publishing – designing surveys/questionnaires
- word processing – creating questionnaires
- Internet – to look at products produced by competitors
- e-mail – send reports/photographs concerning a new product between the food retailer and the food manufacturer
- graph programs – to produce results of questionnaires/sensory analysis
- nutrition programs – to calculate the nutritional value of a product
- spreadsheets – to calculate costs
- paint/draw programs – produce packaging/labelling
- digital camera – provide images for packaging and recording how a product should look
- clipart – create mood boards
- scanner – scanning images onto food packages.

3 Possible answers include:

- linked to machinery that manufactures the food product
- manufacturing of packaging
- printing of labelling information on packaging
- data logging
- stock control.

4 Possible answers include:

Benefits of CAD are:

- speeds up the time of some tasks, for example, drawing
- gives greater accuracy when working out the cost of a product
- gives a professional finished result to packaging
- work can be quickly changed, for example, the design of a package.

Benefits of CAM are:

- saves time. Repetitive tasks can be completed quickly e.g. filling pastry cases
- it increases productivity. More products made at speed means lower costs
- a consistent final product is manufactured
- it increases safety. Machinery rather than workers can carry out more hazardous tasks.

5 Enrober – wraps or coats a product. E.g. biscuits are coated or enrobed with chocolate.
  Depositor – adds fillings to products e.g. fillings to cakes.
  Data logger – monitors weight, temperature, moisture content, pH level of a food product.

Pages 51–52

1 Possible answers include:

Method of production	Description	Examples of products
Job/craft or one-off	Only one product is produced. A quality item which is unique.	Wedding cake, birthday cake.
Batch	A specific amount of a product is made for distribution. Small orders can be made. The machinery can be used to make a variety of products.	Cakes, biscuits, bread.
Repetitive flow	Large numbers of identical products are produced at a low cost. Manufacture takes place on an assembly line.	Sandwich production.
Continual or continuous flow	Computer-controlled. One specific product is manufactured 24 hours per day, 7 days a week producing a high quality product.	Breakfast cereals, crisps, soft drinks, margarine, bread.

2 Possible answers include:
   ● accurate weighing and measuring of ingredients
   ● use same size holes on grater for cheese
   ● use same size cutter
   ● roll out to same depth
   ● cook at same temperature in oven.

3 Bar codes help consumers by:
   ● providing a quicker service at the till
   ● providing an itemised receipt which can easily be checked.

   Bar codes help retailers:
   ● to keep a check of stock
   ● allow faster reordering from the manufacturer.

4 'Best before' date – appears on foods with a short to medium shelf life such as bread, biscuits, crisps and sweets. The day, month and year will be shown.
   'Use by' date – found on chilled products e.g. sandwiches, cook-chill meals. The product must be used by the date stated. If it is not used by this date it should be thrown away. The day and month will be shown.

5 Vegetarian or person on a low-fat diet.
   ● Quorn is a vegetarian product
   ● It is in the form of mince, so it can be used to replace meat in cooking
   ● It is low in fat

6 **a** 7.7g
   b 26.9g
   c 2.9g
   d 1.4g

7 Possible answers include:

- Consumers may have an allergy or intolerance to an additive.
- Some consumers are not happy with certain additives being added to foods for children e.g. E101 causing hyperactivity.
- Some additives previously thought safe have been withdrawn from food products due to evidence clearly indicating problems for some consumers.
- The consumer can make an informed choice.
- Some consumers prefer natural additives to artificial ones.

Page 55

1 Possible answers include:

- allows checks for improvements / modifications to be made to the product, the equipment and the production system
- to ensure the product appeals to the user group
- to make sure the product will sell
- to check portion size
- to keep cost and waste to a minimum
- to identify if a product can be developed further into a range
- to ensure the product meets the design and product specifications
- make sure product fits the brief
- nutritional evaluation
- look at different packaging.

2 Possible answers include:

- the research stage
- the design idea stage
- the trialling and testing stage
- the manufacturing stage
- after sales.

3 Possible answers include:

- cost
- portion size
- nutritional content
- taste
- texture
- appearance
- aroma
- environmentally friendly
- suitable for manufacture in quantity
- suitable shelf life.

Pages 64–66

1 Possible answers include:

- Comparisons of the nutritional content of different products can be made.
- May be on a special diet e.g. low fat/high fibre.
- An informed choice can be made.
- To have a variety of nutrients/balanced diet.
- It may help to decide what to serve with a product. For example, a product may be low in fibre, therefore fibre rich foods need to be added to a meal.

2 Possible answers include;

- textured vegetable protein or TVP
- Quorn^{TM}
- Tofu.

3 Answers could include:

Function	Examples
Glazing	Egg, milk, golden syrup, honey
Sweeten	Sugar, dried fruits, honey, golden syrup, treacle
Bulking	Flour, oats, rice, bread
Thickening	Flour, eggs, potatoes, rice, bread, pasta
Aerating	Eggs, baking powder, yeast
Binding	Water, milk, egg
Setting	Gelatine, eggs, cornflour
Preserving	Salt, sugar, vinegar
Emulsifying	Egg yolk

4 Possible answers could include:
- Honey is used as a glaze – roast ham
- Dried fruits are used to sweeten – breakfast cereals/cakes
- Bread is used as bulk – meat loaf/burgers
- Rice is used as bulk – risotto/paella
- Yeast is used to aerate – bread/cakes
- Egg is used to bind – burgers/fish cakes
- Eggs are used to set – quiche/cakes
- Sugar is used to preserve – jam/marmalade.

5 Possible answers could include:

Ingredient	Function
200g self raising flour	Adds bulk, coats the fat to give an even mixture, raising agents in flour ensure product rises.
50g hard margarine	Adds flavour, adds moisture, prevents flour proteins from joining together.
Pinch of salt	Adds flavour.
50ml milk	Binds mixture together, adds moisture.
50g mature Cheddar cheese	Adds flavour, adds colour. Adds flavour, adds texture.

6 Possible answers include:
- Grated cheese – pizza topping, savoury flan, cheese scones
- Pie fillings – apple pie, meat pie, Cornish pasties
- Jam – jam tarts, sponge pudding, filling for a sponge cake
- Custard – trifle, sponge pudding & custard dessert, cakes

7 Possible answers include:
- People do not like the thought of animals being killed or kept in inhumane conditions.
- Religious beliefs.
- The cost.
- Health risk issues e.g. BSE.
- People believe that a diet without meat is healthier.
- Peer pressure.
- People do not like the taste.

Page 71

1 Hazard Analysis and Critical Control Points.

2 Possible answers include:
- food is bought from reputable suppliers
- food is stored at the correct temperature
- raw and cooked foods are kept separate at all times
- chilling and freezing of food is at the correct temperature
- food is cooked at the correct temperature for correct length of time
- correct cleaning procedures of equipment and premises are put in place
- correct pest control is in place
- staff are trained in food hygiene
- metal detection is in place
- ensuring machinery is working correctly
- stock is rotated
- hot food is kept at the correct temperature
- the weight of a product is accurate
- the size and shape of a product is consistent.

3 Quality assurance is a system that is set up before a product is made and that lays down the procedures for making a safe, quality product.

4 Quality control consists of the steps in the process of making a product to make sure that it meets the standards. Any faulty products are removed.

5 Feedback is used in control systems to see if the output is correct. Information is fed back to ensure all parts of the system are working correctly.

Page 80

1 Answers include:
- the ham
- the chicken legs
- the cream cake.

2 Chicken, fresh stock, rice.

3 Raw meat should be stored at the bottom of the refrigerator to avoid cross contamination. Bacteria from raw meat could be passed onto the cooked meat.

4 In the refrigerator.

5 To avoid cross contamination.

6 raw fish – blue   raw meat – red   fruit and vegetables – green   cooked meat – yellow

Page 84

1 Possible answers include:
They ensure that ...
- food is labelled correctly
- correct weight is shown on a product
- measuring/weighing equipment is accurate by visiting food premises
- food is safe by taking samples from food
- the Food Safety Act (1990) is enforced.

2 Possible answers include:
- buy products that have minimal packaging
- buy organic produce
- buy products where packaging can be recycled
- buy products where packaging is made from recycled materials.

3 No artificial fertilisers, pesticides or intensive growing systems.
Better taste. Better for the environment.